CW01081831

On the Play of the Child

INDICATIONS BY RUDOLF STEINER FOR WORKING WITH YOUNG CHILDREN

Selected and edited by Freya Jaffke

With five lectures from the 2005
International Waldorf Kindergarten Conference
Playing, Learning, Meeting the Other

WECAN
WALDORF EARLY CHILDHOOD
ASSOCIATION OF NORTH AMERICA

On the Play of the Child:
Indications by Rudolf Steiner for Working with Young Children
Second English Edition
© 2012 Waldorf Early Childhood Association of North America
ISBN: 978-1-936849-17-8

First published in German by
the Internationale Vereinigung der Waldorfkindergärten e.V., Stuttgart
as *Vom Spiel des Kindes* and *Spielen, Lernen, Begegnen: Vorträge.*
This book combines the contents of two previous WECAN publications,
On the Play of the Child and *Playing, Learning, Meeting the Other.*

Front cover photo: from a kindergarten classroom at Green Meadow Waldorf
School, Chestnut Ridge, NY. © Natt McFee
Back cover photos: from Awhina Day Nursery and Kindergarten, New Zealand.
Courtesy of Bernadette Raichle

English Edition Editor: Susan Howard
German Edition Editor (*Playing, Learning, Meeting the Other*): Brigitte Goldmann
Managing Editor and Graphic Design: Lory Widmer
Translator: Jan-Kees Saltet

This publication was made possible by a grant from the Waldorf Curriculum
Fund and produced in cooperation with the International Association
for Steiner/Waldorf Early Childhood Education (IASWECE).

Waldorf Early Childhood Association of North America
285 Hungry Hollow Rd.
Spring Valley, NY 10977
845-352-1690
info@waldorfearlychildhood.org
www.waldorfearlychildhood.org

For a complete book catalog, contact WECAN or visit our online store:
store.waldorfearlychildhood.org

Contents

Editor's Note 5

On the Play of the Child 7

Preface 9

Introduction 11

Understanding and Fostering Healthy Creative Play
by Joan Almon 15

The Inner Attitude of the Educator 19

Imitation 23

The Child's Play 25

Toys and Play Materials 49

Creating the Right Environment for the Child 65

References 75

Playing, Learning, Meeting the Other 79

Preface 81

Meeting the Other: The Human Encounter
• *Heinz Zimmermann* 83

The Healing Power of Play • *Joan Almon* 97

Acceleration, Retardation, and Healthy Development
• *Michaela Glöckler* 109

The Formative Forces and the Threshold of the Second Seven-
Year Period • *Christof Wiechert* 121

The Encounter with Human and Spiritual Beings
• *Heinz Zimmermann* 129

Biographical Notes 139

Editor's Note

TO THE 2012 COMBINED EDITION

We are very pleased to offer this new edition of two publications that came into being just before and after the international gathering of Waldorf early childhood educators in Dornach, Switzerland in 2005.

In *On the Play of the Child*, Freya Jaffke has compiled a wonderful resource for early childhood educators and all those interested in the profound significance of free, creative play in the life of the child. This volume was prepared as study material for the 2005 conference and has proved to be a valuable resource ever since.

Playing, Learning, Meeting the Other collects five of the lectures that were given at the 2005 conference, around the themes of play, development and learning, and the all-important encounter with the other.

This April, we once again experienced a gathering of Waldorf early childhood educators from around the world, in our seven-year cycle of conferences at the Goetheanum. At the same time as we were preparing the proceedings from the 2012 conference (published as *The Journey of the 'I' into Life*), we reviewed these older materials. We found that they offer important insights that are of value to educators today, and decided to publish this combined edition. We hope that it will continue to provide inspiration and support for your work for many years to come.

—*Susan Howard, September 2012*

On the Play of the Child

Preface
FROM THE 2004 EDITION

In anticipation of the International Teachers Conference that will be held at the Goetheanum in Dornach during Easter of 2005, the conference planning group of the International Association of Waldorf Kindergartens felt the need for a comprehensive collection of quotations about children's play from the collected works of Rudolf Steiner.

The main theme of the conference will be children's play in the broadest sense of the word. Imaginative play is greatly threatened in our time. Its tremendous significance for the young child and for all of later life will be explored at the conference, and it is hoped that the conference can serve as a focal point for intensive worldwide collaboration on this theme.

It is our hope that the quotations collected in this book will stimulate the reader to explore the context in which they were given. This in turn might give rise to further insights. Familiarity with an anthroposophical image of the human being is a prerequisite for a full understanding of the quotations. At the beginning of this book, which is published both in German and English, the present situation of children's play is described in an article by Joan Almon.

It is my hope that this book will inspire readers and that the many important suggestions contained in it will enrich the daily work of those who carry the responsibility of caring for young children and working together with their parents. I am aware of the fact that a collection of quotations such as this one can never be complete. I would be grateful to receive suggestions for more quotations, which could be incorporated in the next edition.

—*Freya Jaffke, February 2004*

Introduction

Note: All numbers in brackets refer to the reference list on page 75.

The following quotation is one of the most concrete indications that Rudolf Steiner gave concerning the kindergarten. Yet its content is fundamental and poses a challenge to us in regard to the way we do our daily work.

4/18/1923; in *The Child's Changing Consciousness*, reference number [16], pp. 71-72

For the entire life of a preschool class revolves around the children adapting to the few people in charge, who should behave naturally so that the children feel stimulated to imitate whatever their teachers do.

It is unnecessary for preschool staff to go from one child to another and show each one what to do. Children do not yet want to follow given instructions. All they want is to copy what the adult does. The task of the kindergarten teacher is to adjust the work taken from daily life so that it becomes suitable for the children's play activities. The whole point of a preschool is to give young children the opportunity to imitate life in a simple and wholesome way.

A little later in the same lecture it says that this is "an incredibly important pedagogical task" and that it will "take a long time." Hardly any work of this kind had been done at that point (1923!).

In many lecture-cycles for teachers and educators, Rudolf Steiner points to the importance of the first seven years for the whole of human life.

8/10/1923, "Walking, Speaking, Thinking"; in *A Modern Art of Education* [17]

> In true methods of education it can never be a question of considering the child as it is at a given moment, but in relation to the whole of its journey through life from birth to death; for the seed of the whole earthly life is already present in the first years of life.

Rudolf Steiner describes through a variety of new aspects how the little child is a being of imitation. He describes where this capacity for imitation comes from and what consequences this has for educators and for the environment which needs to be created around the child. Many descriptions are given of the young child as a sensory being and also as a being of will, and of how impressions from the environment work on the child.

Every teacher who lives intensively with the various indications given by Rudolf Steiner (also meditatively with certain passages) will notice a growing sense of responsibility towards the children. And it will become clear that education is based, in essence, on self-education. Rudolf Steiner even says:

4/20/1923, *The Child's Changing Consciousness* [16], pp. 141-142

> Essentially, there is no education other than self-education, whatever the level may be. This is recognized in its full depth within anthroposophy, which has conscious knowledge through spiritual investigation of repeated Earth lives. Every education is self-education, and as teachers we can only provide the environment for children's self-education. We have to provide the most favorable conditions where, through our agency, children can educate themselves according to their own destinies. This is the attitude that teachers should have toward children, and such an attitude can be developed only through an ever-growing awareness of this fact.

The passages from Rudolf Steiner's lectures in this book have been compiled mainly with an eye to children's play. They include the following aspects: the seriousness of play; the connection of play and work; the relationship of play to later life and health; and the importance of play materials. As the impulses for play always arise from the environment, some examples of the environment's influence are also included.

Out of his deep knowledge of the human being and his spiritual research, Rudolf Steiner was able to shed light on a variety of aspects in education. Apart from very important specific indications concerning different play materials, he was able to only give a few indications for the daily practice in the kindergarten. This task was taken up intensively when a kindergarten was started (after Steiner's death). This was accomplished, above all, by Elizabeth Grunelius, whom Steiner himself had asked to do this.

During the past eighty years of the twentieth century, there have been several books and articles written by Waldorf early childhood educators. The authors of these publications have been able to point out detailed perceptions, for example, concerning the different stages of the freeing of the etheric forces in the child, the importance of the maternal etheric sheath, the play of the child, play and work, the creation of surroundings with appropriate play materials, ways to nurture the will of the child, and many other things.

Even though much has been accomplished in producing literature up to now, there is still plenty for the next generations of early childhood educators to do. It is also important to reexamine our own experiences and deepen them with the help of the anthroposophical study of the human being.

Understanding and Fostering Healthy Creative Play BY JOAN ALMON

Play is a fundamental activity of childhood, and the playful child is generally viewed as a healthy, active child. After a child has been ill, parents will often describe the seriousness of the illness in terms of whether the child was still able to play. "She was really sick and couldn't play at all," or "He was sick but was up playing," are comments often heard from parents. There is scientific research to support this view, showing that play is linked to children's healthy physical, social, emotional and mental development. The absence of play becomes a serious problem in children's lives.

There are many types of play, ranging from simple play where young children handle materials such as pots and pans and other household objects, to make-believe play where two or more children play out complex stories together. This can be in a single play session or over many days. One sees the same types of play among children all over the world, and one can speak of a common language of play. Children from different cultures, for example, can happily play together without knowing a single word of one another's spoken language.

At the same time, one sees differences according to children's age and development, their gender, and individual nature. Culture also plays a role. Among cultural differences, for instance, one sees that European children playing mother will push their dolls in prams, while in Africa they tie their baby dolls onto their backs with colorful cloths. Children imitate what they see around them and at the same time play bubbles up from deep inner wellsprings.

Even in situations of war or poverty, most children continue to play, although children suffering from serious illness or trauma may stop playing, at least for a time. What does it mean, then, that one hears in the U.S. and elsewhere that play is disappearing from childhood—that there is no time for play or that children have forgotten how to play? There are rising rates of physical and mental illness among children, and it may well be that this is related directly or indirectly to the loss of play. The World Health Organization, for instance, has sounded an alarm that mental illness among children may increase by 50% by the year 2020. At the same time, many countries are concerned about the increases in childhood obesity and related illnesses. Because play is so linked to children's healthy development, its absence must be taken seriously.

Waldorf early childhood educators have recognized the disappearance of play from childhood for some time, but increasingly we hear concern from other educators, psychologists, and doctors. A child psychiatrist in the U.S., for example, recently wrote of a 50% reduction in children's play over the past twenty years. Interviews with experienced kindergarten teachers in the U.S. brought forward two common answers: there was considerably less time in their curriculum for play now than ten years ago, and when they gave children time to play, the children did not know what to do. A professor whose area of study is play noted a similar response. She asked early childhood educators in a workshop how many had children in their kindergartens who did not know how to play. About 90% of the 200 teachers raised their hands. Experts are beginning to speak out about these problems in an effort to alert parents, educators, doctors and government officials. Organizations are also forming which are focusing on the importance of play, such as the Alliance for Childhood.

One naturally asks why play is disappearing, and there seem to be several answers. One is the amount of media children watch, and this includes television, films, and computer time. The average time for a child in the U.S. to sit still in front of a screen is now between four and five hours per day outside of school time. This is time when children are not engaged in play, but it is also time when children are absorbing other people's images. This limits the development of their own imagination.

Another factor is the growing emphasis on early learning. Using the U.S. as an example, five-year-olds are often attending all-day kindergartens where they may spend 90 minutes a day on early reading, 60 minutes on mathematics, and devote time each day to science and social studies activities yet have no time for indoor play. Five-year-olds in many places in the U.S. are expected to enter kindergarten knowing their alphabet, basic sounds, numbers and much more. To prepare children for this, most pre-schools focus on teaching academics to three- and four-year-olds. Often, young children are tested on what they have learned in these early years so the stress on academic achievement becomes considerable.

A third factor is the growing amount of time young children spend in or-ganized activities rather than in child-initiated play. Many young children are taking classes in gymnastics, sports, dance, music and other subjects. Some attend several classes a week after they return from their regular pre-school programs, leaving almost no time for unstructured play.

Perhaps the greatest consideration is that parents feel a need to see their children get ahead in life and push intellectual awareness and organized activities from the earliest ages, undervaluing play and discouraging children from engaging in it. Early childhood educators frequently complain that parents are insisting that the teachers push early academics even though they, the teachers, do not think the children need this push. Reaching the parents to help them understand the critical role of play in their child's healthy development is probably the most important single step we can take in bringing play back into children's lives.

An additional consideration with play is the role of imitation in stimulat-ing play. Children need to see adults engaged in meaningful work, for it inspires children to play. Yet today's children see very little real work in their environment. When helping children who can't play, it is astonish-ing how quickly play can be reactivated once children are exposed to real work, whether it is cooking, gardening, carpentry or the like.

The absence of play can have serious consequences for the development of a child's imagination and creativity. Without play children are less likely to be able to form their own independent ideas. This in turn can have an impact on society, for democracies rely on citizens being able to think creatively and independently. On the other hand, totalitarian regimes do not tolerate such independent thinking and strive to hinder its development. If one wants to prepare children for life in an active and thriving democratic state, then it is critical that we help them play creatively when they are young.

For all of these reasons it has become very important that people recog-nize the vital role of play and do all they can to bring play back into child-hood. The insights of Rudolf Steiner regarding play and the experiences in Waldorf kindergartens can be a great help in awakening an understanding of play and in inspiring us all to work on behalf of play.

The Inner Attitude of the Educator

Before proceeding to the quotations concerning play and play materials, we will include some passages of Rudolf Steiner's lectures here with guidelines concerning the appropriate inner attitude that we must foster as educators.

We hear about the child's divine spiritual being seeking to find a connection here on earth to a physical sheath. Here the most significant help for the child is the presence of the adult in its surroundings who has an appropriate inner attitude for in the kindergarten it is not so much the educational program that counts, but the inner attitude of the teachers.

08/11/1923 "The Rhythmic System, Sleeping and Waking, Imitation"; in *A Modern Art of Education* [17]

True observation of man sees in the growing human being a work of divine creation. There is no more wonderful spectacle in the whole world than to see in the child how, from birth on, the definite gradually emerges from the indefinite in the body, how seemingly meaningless, undefined, arbitrary movements, change into movements determined by the soul, how more and more the inner being expresses itself outwardly, and the spiritual element in the body comes gradually to the surface. This being which the divine world has sent down to earth, and which we feel is revealing itself in the body, becomes a revelation of the Divine itself. The growing human being is indeed its most splendid manifestation.

If we learn to know this growing human being, not from the point of view of ordinary anatomy and physiology, but with an understanding of how the soul and spirit stream down into the body, then all our knowledge of man changes into religion, into truly devout and humble reverence in the face of what streams into the surface of things from out of divine depths. Then, as teachers, we have a certain quality that bears and sustains us, and that becomes for the child a natural authority in which he places spontaneous trust.

04/09/1924; in *The Essentials of Education* [18], pp. 24-25

Few things have a more wonderful effect on the human heart than seeing inner spirit and soul elements released day to day, week to week, month to month, year to year, during the first period of childhood. We see how, beginning with chaotic movements of the limbs, a gaze that focuses on superficial outer stimuli and facial expressions that do not yet seem to belong to the child, something is developing and impressing itself on the surface of the human form, something that arises from the center of the human being, where the divine spiritual being is unfolding in its descent from pre-earthly life.

Waldorf Education and Anthroposophy 2 [14], pp. 131-132

When entering earthly life, human beings not only receive what is passed on by heredity through their fathers and mothers, but they also descend as spirit beings from the spiritual worlds into this earthly world. This fact can be applied practically in education when we have living insight into the human being. Basically, I cannot think of impressions more wonderful that those received while observing a young baby develop if we participate inwardly in such a gradual unfolding. After the infant has descended from the spiritual world into the earthly world, we can observe what was blurred and indistinct at first, gradually taking on form and shape.

If we follow this process, we feel direct contact with the spiritual world, which is incarnating and unfolding before our very eyes, right here in the sensory world. Such an experience provides a sense of responsibility toward one's tasks as a teacher, and with the necessary care, the art of education attains the quality of a religious service. Then, amid all our practical tasks, we feel that the gods themselves have sent the human being into this earthly existence, and they have entrusted the child to us for education. With the incarnating child, the gods have given us enigmas that inspire the most beautiful divine service.

04/08/1924; in *The Essentials of Education* [18], p. 14

For the small child before the change of teeth, the most important thing in education is the teacher's own being.

04/08/1924; in *The Essentials of Education* [18], p. 13-14

The most important considerations have to do with the kind of person one is, what impressions the child receives, and whether or not one is worthy of imitation.

Imitation

All play and activity of the child is based on imitation. In the majority of quotations below, Rudolf Steiner describes how the young child functions entirely as a sense organ during the first phase of life. Steiner shows us what and how the child, up to approximately age seven, imitates, and he does this in a variety of ways.

To begin with, we will give a few quotations that guide us into the realms where imitation originates. Imitation here on earth is a continuation of a habit formed in the spiritual world.

08/09/1919; in *Education As a Force for Social Change* [8], p. 11

Children carry their prenatal experiences in the spiritual world into physical existence after birth. In the spiritual world, we human beings live in the beings of the higher hierarchies; everything we do arises out of the nature of the higher hierarchies. There, we are imitative to a much greater extent because we are united with those beings we imitate. Then we are placed into the physical world, but we continue our habit of being at one with our surroundings. The habit of being at one with the beings in our surroundings, of imitating them, continues. We continue to imitate those who are responsible for our upbringing and who are to do and feel only what we should imitate. It is extremely healthy for children to be able to live not so much in their own souls, but in the souls of the people around them. . .

In the future, we must attend to the fact that the child's behavior is imitative. In raising children, we need to continuously keep in mind how we can best create the most favorable environment for their imitative behavior. Everything done in the past regarding imitation must become more and more conscious and more and more consciously connected with the future. People will need to remind themselves that if children are to grow up to meet the needs of the social organism, they must be free. People become free only if they were intensively imitative as children. We need to intensely develop the strength, the natural strength, of children in preparation for that time when they begin to become socially interactive. In spite of all political complaining about freedom, and in spite of all the other talk, people will become free only if we ingrain the strength of imitation in them during childhood. Only what we thus implant during childhood can serve as a basis for social freedom.

04/16/1924, in *The Roots of Education* [19], p. 60

Only on the basis of this knowledge can we correctly understand what expresses itself in the life and activities of children under seven. They simply continue in their earthly life a tendency of soul that was the most essential aspect of life before birth. In the spiritual realm, one surrenders completely to the spirit all around, lives outside oneself, all the more individually, yet outside of one's self. One wants to continue this tendency toward devotion in earthly life—wants to continue in the body the activity of pre-earthly life in the spiritual worlds. This is why the whole life of a small child is naturally religious.

10/12/1917; in *The Fall of the Spirits of Darkness* [7]

And if they do not imitate sufficiently they will not have enough in them later that they can use.

The Child's Play

For orientation, short indications are given for this chapter as to the content of the various quotes on children's play.

p. 27   The task of the kindergarten (04/18/1924 [16])

p. 29   The nature of play demands true insight into the being of the child, play and imitation; bring nothing of an intellectual nature into the child's play (08/10/1923 [17])

p. 32   Playing means being active in soul and spirit; the connection of play with the time after age twenty in a human biography. Responsibility of the educator in leading play activity. (06/10/1920 [23])

p. 34   The essence of playing is based in the fact that we leave the child to its own resources. *No firm rules*. Don't bring in anything intellectual. (03/14/1912 [5])

p. 35   Play in the first years springs from a deep awareness of the essential nature of the human being. (01/12/1911 [4])

p. 36   The connection of play with the temperament disposition of the child. (12/29/1920 [9])

p. 36   Let play only be imitation of life. (08/13/1924 [21])
p. 37   (08/19/1924 [21])

p. 38   Play will only represent an imitation of adult activity, no practical value yet; "The human being is only truly human as long as he plays." (Schiller). Play and dream activity. Fruits of play after the twentieth year. (05/10/1920 [12])

p. 41   The relationship of play to the time after the age of twenty. (01/13/1921 [10])

p. 42   (12/29/1920 [9])

p. 43   Acquire an artistic sense for the way a child plays. (02/24/1921 [25])

p. 44   For the child, play is a serious occupation; for the grownup, play is for relaxation. (03/25/1923 [14])

p. 45   How do we create the bridge between the joy of play and the burden of life's work? (03/25/1923 [14])

p. 46   Connection of play and health and later life. (04/14/1924 [19]) (08/24/1922 [15])

p. 47   (04/14/1924 [19])

p. 47   Don't introduce stereotypical forms of play to the child. (01/06/1922 [13])

p. 47   Should preschool have the character of kindergarten? (06/14/1920 [11])

04/18/1924; in *The Child's Changing Consciousness* [16], pp. 70-73

Generally speaking, education has followed in the footsteps of our modern civilization, which has gradually become more and more materialistic. A symptom of this is the frequent use of mechanical methods in preference to organic methods, and this just during the early years of childhood up to the change of teeth, which is the most impressionable and important time of life. We must not lose sight of the fact that, up to the second dentition, the child lives by imitation. The serious side of life, with all of its demands in our daily work, is reenacted in deep earnestness by the child in its play. . .The difference between a child's play and an adult's work is that an adult's contribution to society is governed by a sense of purpose and has to fit into outer demands, whereas the child wants to be active simply out of an inborn and natural impulse. Play activity streams outward from within. Adult work takes the opposite direction, namely inwards from the periphery. . .

. . .In their play, children mirror what happens around them; they want to imitate. But because the key to childhood has been lost through inadequate knowledge of the human being, adults have intellectually contrived all kinds of artificial play activities for children of kindergarten age. Since children want to imitate the work of the adults, special games have been invented for their benefit, such as "Pick-up Sticks," or whatever else these things are called. These artificial activities actually deflect the child's inner forces from flowing out of the organism as a living stream that finds a natural outlet in the child's desire to imitate those who are older. Through all kinds of mechanical manipulations, children are encouraged to do things not at all suitable to their age. Particularly during the nineteenth century, there were programs for preschool education that involved activities a child should not really do; for the entire life of a preschool class revolves around the children adapting to the few people in charge, who should behave naturally so that the children feel stimulated to imitate whatever their teachers do.

It is unnecessary for preschool staff to go from one child to another and show each one what to do. Children do not yet want to follow given instructions. All they want is to copy what the adult does, so the task of a kindergarten teacher is to adjust the work taken from daily life so that it becomes suitable for the children's play activities. There is no need to devise occupations like those adults meet in life, except under special circumstances such as work that requires specialized skills. For example, children of preschool age are told to make parallel cuts in strips of paper and then to push multi-colored paper strips through the slits so that a woven colored pattern finally emerges. This kind of mechanical process in a kindergarten actually prevents children from engaging in normal or congenial activities. It would be better to give them some very simple sewing or embroidery to do. Whatever a young child is told to do should not be artificially contrived by adults who are comfortable in our intellectual culture, but should arise from the tasks of ordinary life. The whole point of a preschool is to give young children the opportunity to imitate life in a simple and wholesome way.

This task of adjusting life as one carries it out in the presence of the child in a meaningful, purposeful way, according to the needs of the child, is in accordance with the child's natural and inborn need for activity and is an enormously significant educational task. To contrive little stick games or design paper weaving cards is simple. But it is a tremendously important and necessary task to adapt and transform our complicated ways of life, such as a child does when, for example, a little boy plays with a spade or some other tool, or when a girl plays with a doll; in this way children transform adult occupations into child's play, including the more complicated activities of the adult world. This is a challenging task for which hardly any previous "spade-work" has thus far been done. One needs to recognize that in children's imitation, in all their sense-directed activities, moral and spiritual forces are working, artistic impulses that allow the child to respond in an entirely individual way.

Give a child a handkerchief or a piece of cloth, knot it so that a head appears above and two legs below, and you have made a doll or a kind of clown. With a few ink spots you can give it eyes, nose, and mouth, or even better, allow the child to do it, and with such a doll, you will see a healthy child have great joy. Now the child can add many other features belonging to a doll, through imagination and imitation within the soul. It is far better if you make a doll out of a linen rag than if you give the child one of those perfect dolls, possibly with highly colored cheeks and smartly dressed, a doll that even closes its eyes when put down horizontally, and so on. What are you doing if you give the child such a doll? You are preventing the unfolding of the child's own soul activity. Every time a completely finished object catches its eye, the child has to suppress an innate desire for soul activity, the unfolding of a wonderfully delicate, awakening fantasy. You thus separate children from life, because you hold them back from their own inner activity.

08/10/1923; in *A Modern Art of Education* [17]

If we would give loving help to the child at play we must realize how many inner, formative forces are active in his being. In this respect our whole civilization is on the wrong road. . .

. . .The first great essential is to learn to deal with them lovingly, and lovingly give them only what their own beings demand. We should not inflict inner punishments by giving the child toys of the type of the "beautiful" doll. We should be able to live with the child and fashion dolls that the child himself inwardly experiences.

Thus play also is something that calls for true insight into the nature of the child. If we babble like small infants and think to bring our speech down to their level, if we do not speak in a genuine way in which the child can experience that our speech is genuinely coming out of our inner being, we bring an untruthful influence to bear upon the child. On the other hand, however, we must be able to descend to the stage of the child's development in everything that has to do with the will-nature, in everything that goes into his play. We shall then realize that intellectuality—a quality so much admired in our modern age—simply does not exist in the child's organic nature, and should, therefore, have no place in his play. The child at play will naturally imitate what is going on in his surroundings, but it will seldom happen that a child of four expresses a wish to be, let us say, a philologist, although he may say he would like to be a chauffeur! Why? This is because everything a chauffeur does can be seen. It makes a direct pictorial impression. It is different with a philologist, for what he does makes no such impression; it is non-pictorial, it simply passes by unnoticed by the child. In play, however, we must introduce only what does not pass by the child unnoticed. Everything intellectual leaves the child unaffected, it passes him by. What, then, must we adults do if we are to help the child to the right kind of play?

Now when we plow, make hats, or sew clothes, and so on, all these things are done with a certain purpose, and the intellectual element lies in this purposefulness. When we discern the purpose of something in life, we penetrate it intellectually. But everything in life—no matter whether it be plowing, building carriages, shoeing horses, or the like, besides having a definite purpose, contains another element in outward appearance, something that lives in its sheer outward appearance. At the sight of a man guiding his plow over the field, one can feel—apart from the object of plowing—what one might call the sculptural, formative quality of the activity, which lives in its image, which becomes a picture. If we struggle through to a feeling for this pictorial, formative element—quite apart from its purpose—(and it is our aesthetic sense that enables us to do this)—then we can begin to make toys that really appeal to the child. We shall not aim at intellectual beauty (as in the modern doll), but at something expressed in the whole movement, in the whole feeling of the human being. Then, instead of the "beautiful" doll, we shall produce a primitive, truly enchanting doll something like this one, but that is already something for older children! [1]

Therefore, in order to become true educators, the essential thing is to be able to see the truly aesthetic element in the work, to bring an artistic quality into our tasks, such as the creation of play materials. If we apply this aesthetic element to the process of making play materials, we then begin to come closer to what the child wills out of its own nature.

Our civilization has made us, with very few exceptions, wholly utilitarian and intellectualistic, and we what offer our children is the result of what we have "thought out" with our brains. But we ought not to give them what adult life has thought out, but rather what can be felt and experienced in later life. This is what the play materials should express. If we make a child a toy plow, the essential thing is that it should express the aesthetic-formative quality of plowing, for this will help to unfold the full forces of the human being.

Certain kindergartens, worthy in other ways of great recognition and respect, have made great mistakes in this regard. Kindergartens developed by Froebel and others out of true inner love for children have failed to realize that imitation is a part of the very nature of the child, who can only imitate that which is not yet permeated by an intellectual quality. We must therefore not introduce into the kindergarten such various forms of handwork as have been ingeniously "thought out." The arranging of sticks, basketwork and so on, that play so large a part in modern kindergarten methods, have

---

1 Dr. Steiner here showed a doll made by pupils of the Waldorf School.

all been ingeniously thought out. Kindergarten work ought rather to be arranged so that it contains an actual picture of what older people do, and not mere inventions. A sense of tragedy will often arise in one possessed of a true knowledge of man upon entering one of these modern kindergartens—for they are so full of good intentions and the work has been so conscientiously thought out. They are based on infinite goodwill and a sincere love of children, yet they have not realized that all intellectualism (everything that has been only thought out) ought to be eliminated. Kindergarten work should consist simply and solely of the external imitation of the external picture of what grown-up people do.

A child whose intellectual faculties are developed before the fourth or fifth year bears a dreadful heritage into later life. He will simply become a materialist. To the extent that an intellectual education is given to the child before the fourth or fifth year will he become materialistic in later life. For the brain is so worked on that the intellectually spiritual takes hold of it, lives in its forms. The human being, because this process has taken place too soon, comes to the view that everything is just material.

If we would so train the child that as a human being he may comprehend the spirit, then we must delay as long as possible bringing that which is outwardly spiritual in its purely intellectual form. Although it is highly necessary, in view of the nature of our modern civilization, that each person should be fully awake in later life, the child must be allowed to remain as long as possible in the peaceful, dreamlike condition of pictorial imagination in which his early years are passed. For if we allow his organism to grow strong in this non-intellectual way, he will rightly develop in later life the intellectuality needed in the world today.

If the child's brain has been flogged in the way I have described, permanent injury is done to the soul. Just as the use of baby-language adversely affects the digestion, just as unloving, misguided coercion in the process of learning to walk has an unfavorable effect upon the metabolic system in later life, so the flogging of the child in this way from within harms the soul. It must be a primary aim of education to do away with this flogging of the soul (the so-called "beautiful" doll) which is also a flogging of the inner physical being because the child is a being of body, soul and spirit, and in order to bring the play of children on to its proper level.

06/10/1920, in GA 335, *Education in the Face of the Present-day World Situation*, not published in English [23]. Translated by JKS.

We see how children devote themselves to play during the first years of their lives. Giving direction and guidance to play is one of the essential tasks of sensible education, which is to say of an art of education that is right for humanity. The child plays. When one has sharpened one's observation of the world and human life. . . one will notice the difference between the way different children play: it varies from one child to the next. To a superficial observer, almost all children play in a similar way. On closer scrutiny, one will notice that each child plays in a different way. Children's play is quite individual. It is a remarkable thing to observe how playing in childhood means engaging in soul and spirit in a way that can only happen when the power of thought is still working within the organism, as is the case up to the time of the change of teeth. It is truly remarkable to see how the child's soul and spirit are active in free play. The element of thought has not yet been absorbed. And it is a kind of play which comes into being without any notion of use or practicality; it is the kind of play in which the child only follows what comes from within. This seems to contradict the principle of imitation. The way the child lives into play originates in the freedom of the child's soul, but only seemingly so. For when one observes more exactly, one will see how children incorporate everything they experience in the world they live in. Everything that is going on around the child is put into the play activity. When one has sharpened one's powers of observation in this respect, one will no longer look upon play of this kind as something interesting, something which just happens in a certain phase of the child's life. One will put playing in perspective and view its character in the context of a total biography.

Only then, by learning through comparison, will one learn to observe what is taking place in the different phases of a human life. In the mineral world, one can compare zinc and copper. In the animal world, one can compare, say, a June bug to a ladybug. All kinds of comparisons of this kind can be made. In exactly the same way one can compare the different stages of human life to one another. When we have developed an eye for this in the way characterized today, we will discover something highly remarkable. We will discover the consequences of children's play for later stages of life. We will see the outcome of the particular character of play, and what it leads to later on in life. Using tangible experiences as a starting point, one is led to the phase of life that lies more or less between the ages of twenty-one and twenty-eight, the time of life during which people find their way into the world and have to grapple with real-life experience. This is when one takes one's first steps towards becoming independent and comes up against life. This phase constitutes a metamorphosis of the particular character of the way a person used to play as a child. Before the change of teeth, the child has freely created out of its own soul activity, using dolls and other play materials; a certain pattern or structure of activity became visible there. When one has learned to discern and recognize this, one will see how characteristic traits return between the ages of twenty and thirty. What became visible as play characteristics during early childhood can be recognized in the way a person acts when confronted with the demands of real life. When a person comes up against serious things in terms of what works and does not work in life; when faced with matters of usefulness and practicality: in those circumstances we can see a reemerging of an attitude which showed itself in free play earlier on.

Just think what this means. We want to educate effectively and know: you observe a characteristic disposition in the play of a child; you guide and direct it now and this will bear fruit twenty years from now, when this person will be coming to terms with the world, a world which should be useful to him and in which he should find his proper place. Just think what feelings arise in the soul of the early childhood educator, who realizes: what I accomplish with this child, I accomplish for the grown-up person in his twenties. What matters here is not so much a knowledge of abstract educational principles, or pedagogical rules which one can produce from an intellectual basis to determine didactic steps. What does matter is that a deep sense of responsibility develops in our hearts when we view life in this way. Real knowledge of the human being does not only speak to our intellects; it speaks to both our hearts and minds and affects our worldview and the way we stand in life. It moves us through and through and works right into our sense of responsibility as teachers. We are not merely looking for an art of education that cleverly calculates the most effective educational methods that could be applied, but we are searching for an art of education which is such that it truly meets the human condition of our time, and which acts on the basis of true insight into the nature of the human being. Such knowledge gives us a sense of responsibility that is, at the same time, a social sense of responsibility towards the whole of humanity. The art of education springs from fundamental feelings, which can only arise in us from a true view of the world.

03/14/1912; in GA 61. *Self-education: The Self-development Of Man in the Light of Anthroposophy.* **Not published in English, but available in typescript from the Rudolf Steiner Library, Ghent, New York [5]**

Thus spiritual science reflects the pattern of a being that includes a higher self, just as in joy and compassion we include others without losing our identity. And as we are aware of our larger self through our ability to enter into the essential being of others, so in the case of the child, apart from what we can draw upon as teachers and what grows and matures out of normal consciousness, we can say that, distinct from the normal self, a higher being exists that is already working upon the child. When we reflect upon this we find something that is exercising a special kind of formative influence on the child, whilst with our orthodox education we can only appeal to the personal self of the child. Where do we find that which acts upon the child as a higher self, as a higher entity that is part of the child, yet never enters into his consciousness? Strange as it may seem, it is nonetheless a fact that this begins to be manifested in purposeful, well-organized play. In the child's play activity, we can only furnish the conditions for education. What is gained through play activity stems fundamentally from the self-activity of the child, through everything that cannot be determined by fixed rules. The real educational value of play lies in the fact that we ignore our rules and regulations, our educational theories, and allow the child free rein.

What does the child do when left to its own devices? In play, the child experiments with external objects in order to find out whether or not they respond to his own activity: he generates an act of will. Through the way in which the external objects respond to the operation of the will, the child learns from life, if only through play, in a totally different way than normally follows from the influence of another personality and his pedagogical principles. Therefore, it is of primary importance that we introduce a minimum of the rationale into the child's play—the less rational and the more imaginative element the play activity, the better. Therefore, when we give the child a toy where the illusion of the movement of people and things is created by pulling strings or some such device, whether it be a child's picture book with mechanical figures of people and animals or some other kind of toy, we educate the child better through free play than when we give it the most finished building blocks. For the latter are too rationally conceived and reflect the more personal element than the more imaginative play materials, where the child tentatively explores the living, creative potentialities, not rationally, but intuitively. [2]

To a certain extent, play activity is an important factor in education for our whole life.

01/12/1911, "Interests, Talent, and Education"; in *The Education of the Child* [4], pp. 96-97

The human instinct for education has created a wonderful common means of enabling young children to work on changing, modifying, and mobilizing what lives in their spirit-soul, thus providing free space for the formation of human nature. What that means is play. That is also the way we can best occupy a child. We should not give children concepts with fixed boundaries, but rather ideas that allow the freedom to think about them, so that children can err here and there. That is the only way we can find the predestined path of thinking arising from each child's innate interest. Tell a fairy tale to excite the child's mental activity. Do not tell it so that fixed concepts develop, but so that the concepts remain flexible. A child will then work the way someone works who tries this and that, and by trying tries to discover what is proper.

A child works to discover how the spirit must move to best shape his or her particular constitution according to inner predetermination. That is how play works. Play differs from activities with more fixed forms because children can still, to a certain extent, do what they want when playing. From the start, play has no clearly defined contours in the children's thoughts, nor any clearly defined movement in their organs. Through play, children have a free but definable manner of acting upon the human soul constitution. Play and the accompanying soul activity of the young child arise from a deep consciousness of what truly constitutes the nature and essence of the human being.

---

2 Further quotations on play materials can be found in the section "Toys and Play Materials."

12/29/1920; in GA 297, *The Spirit of the Waldorf School* [9]; the quote below is from the answer to a question asked after the lecture, which has not been included in the English edition. Translated by JKS.

One will be dealing with the play of very young children. The way a child plays is most characteristic of the individual child before approximately age five. Of course, children also play after that age, but all kinds of other things will be mixed in and play no longer flows as completely from inner arbitrariness, if I may call it that. If one wants to effectively lead play, one will have to develop an eye for what we call the temperament disposition of the child, and other things that are connected to temperaments in children. People usually think that a child that displays a phlegmatic's character should be put on the right track by something lively and stimulating. Likewise, when people are faced with a child which is disposed to be introspective or melancholic in temperament, which may not be there yet as such, but be there as a disposition, they would like to steer such a child in the right direction with something cheerful. This is basically not a very correct way to think about it, especially where play is concerned.

On the contrary, one should try to study the basic character of the child, for instance, find out whether it is a slow or a fast child, and then try to adapt the play to what one finds. So one should try to keep the slow tempo also in play when dealing with a slow child, and keep a fast tempo when dealing with a fast child and only gradually lead on to a transition from that. One should meet the child with exactly that which springs from his or her inner being. People make the worst mistakes in education when they think that like should not be treated with like, but that the right treatment would be to bring opposites together.

08/13/1924; in *The Kingdom of Childhood* [21], p. 18-19

But all the things that you are usually advised to do with kindergarten children are quite worthless. The things that are introduced as kindergarten education are usually extraordinarily "clever." You could be quite fascinated by the cleverness of what has been thought out for kindergartens in the course of the nineteenth century. The children certainly learn a great deal there, they almost learn to read. They are supplied with letters of the alphabet that they have to fit into cut out letters. It all looks very clever and you can easily be tempted to believe that it really is something suitable for children, but it is of no use at all. It really has no value whatsoever, and the soul of the child is impaired by it. The child is damaged even down into the body, right down into physical health. Such kindergarten methods breed weaklings in body and soul for later life.[3]

On the other hand, if you simply have the children there in the kindergarten and conduct yourselves so that they can imitate you, if you do all kinds of things that the children can copy out of their own inner impulse of soul, as they had been accustomed to do in pre-earthly existence, then indeed the children will become like yourself, but it is for you to see that you are worthy of this imitation. This is what you must pay attention to during the first seven years of life and not what you express outwardly in words as a moral idea.

If you make a surly face so that a child gets the impression you are a grumpy person, this harms the child for the rest of his life. This is why it is so important, especially for little children, that, as a teacher, you should enter very thoroughly into the observation of a human being and human life. What kind of school plan you make is neither here nor there; what matters is what sort of a person you are. In our day it is easy enough to think out a curriculum, because everyone in our age is now so clever. I am not saying this ironically; in our day people really are clever. Whenever a few people get together and decide that this or that must be done in education, something clever always comes out of it. I have never known a stupid educational program; they are always very clever. But what is important is that you have people in the school that can work in the way I have indicated. You must develop this way of thinking, for an immense amount depends upon it, especially for that age or life epoch of children in which they are really entirely a sense organ.

08/19/1924; in *The Kingdom of Childhood* [21], p. 118

Herein lies the root of all evil in much of the education of today, and you find, for instance, in the "exemplary" kindergartens that different kinds of work are thought out for the child to do. In reality, we should not allow the children to do anything, even in play, that is not an imitation of life itself. All Froebel occupations and the like, which

---

3 Translator's Note: In Germany, the children remain in the "kindergarten" until their seventh year, so that the above remarks apply to all school life up to this time, including, for instance, the "Infants" departments of state schools in England.

have been thought out for the children, are really bad. We must make it a rule only to let the children do what is an imitation of life, even in play. This is extremely important.

05/10/1920, "Children's Play"; in *The Renewal of Education* [12], pp. 216-221

We need to see how one stage of life affects another. . .When a child is long past school age, has perhaps long since reached adulthood, this is when we can see what school has made of the child and what it has not. This is visible, not only in a general abstract way, but also in a very concrete way.

Let us look at child's play from this perspective, particularly the kind of play that occurs in the youngest child from birth until the change of teeth. Of course, the play of such children is, in one respect, based upon their desire to imitate. Children do what they see adults doing, only they do it differently. They play in such a way that their activities lie far from the goals and utility that adults connect with certain activities. Children's play only imitates the form of adult activities, not the material content. The usefulness in and connection to everyday life are left out. Children perceive a kind of satisfaction in activities that are closely related to those of adults. We can look into this further and ask what is occurring here. If we want to study what is represented by play activities and, through that study, recognize true human nature so that we can have a practical effect upon it, then we must continuously review the individual activities of the child, including those that are transferred to the physical organs and, in a certain sense, form them. That is not so easy. Nevertheless, the study of children's play in the widest sense is extraordinarily important for education.

We need only recall what a person who set the tone for culture once said: "A human being is only a human being so long as he or she plays; and a human being plays so long as he or she is a whole human being." Schiller wrote these words in a letter after he had read some sections of Goethe's *Wilhelm Meister*. . .

. . .We could also, however, compare this kind of play with other human activities. We could, for example, compare children's play before the change of teeth with dreaming, where we most certainly will find some important analogies. However, those analogies are simply related to the course of the child's play, to the connection of the activities to one another in play. In just the same way that children put things together in play—whatever those might be—not with external things but with thoughts, we put pictures together in dreams. This may not be true of all dreams, but it is certainly so in a very large class of them. In dreaming, we remain in a certain sense children throughout our entire lives.

Nevertheless, we can only achieve a genuine understanding if we do not simply dwell upon this comparison of play with dreams. Instead, we should also ask when in the life of the human being something occurs that allows those forces that are developed in early children's play up until the change of teeth, bear fruit for the entirety of external human life. In other words, when do we actually reap the fruits of children's play? Usually people think we need to seek the fruits of young children's play in the period of life that immediately follows, but spiritual science shows how life passes in a rhythmical series of repetitions. In a plant, leaves develop from a seed; from the leaves, the bud and flower petals emerge, and so forth. Only afterwards do we have a seed again; that is, the repetition occurs only after an intervening development. It is the same in human life.

From many points of view we could understand human life as though each period were affected only by the one preceding, but this is not the case. If we observe without prejudice, we will find that the actual fruits of those activities that occur in early childhood play become apparent only at the age of twenty. What we gain in play from birth until the change of teeth, what children experience in a dreamy way, are forces of the still-unborn spirituality of the human being, which is still not yet absorbed into, or perhaps more properly said, reabsorbed into the human body.

We can state this differently. I have already discussed how the same forces that act organically upon the human being until the change of teeth become, when the teeth are born, an independent imaginative or thinking capacity, so that in a certain sense something is removed from the physical body. On the other hand, what is active within a child through play and has no connection with life and contains no usefulness is something that is not yet fully connected with the human body. Thus a child has an activity of the soul that is active within the body until the change of teeth and then becomes apparent as a capacity for forming concepts that can be remembered.

The child also has a spiritual-soul activity that, in a certain sense, still hovers in an etheric way over the child. It is active in play in much the same way that dreams are active throughout the child's entire life. In children, however, this activity occurs not simply in dreams, it occurs also in play, which develops in external reality. What thus develops in external reality subsides in a certain sense. In just the same way that the seed-forming forces of a plant subside in the leaf and flower petal and only reappear in the fruit, what a child uses in play also only reappears at about the age of twenty-one or twenty-two, as independent reasoning gathering experiences in life.

I would like to ask you to try to genuinely seek this connection. Look at children and try to understand what is individual in their play: try to understand the individuality of children playing freely until the change of teeth, and then form pictures of their individualities. Assume that what you notice in their play will become apparent in their independent reasoning after the age of twenty. This means the various kinds of human beings differ in their independent reasoning after the age of twenty in the just the same way that children differ in their play before the change of teeth.

If you recognize the full truth of this thought, you will be overcome by an unbounded feeling of responsibility in regard to teaching. You will realize that what you do with a child forms the human being be-yond the age of twenty. You will see that you will need to understand the entirety of life, not simply the life of children, if you want to cre-ate a proper education.

Playing activity from the change of teeth until puberty is something else again. (Of course, things are not so rigidly separated, but if we want to understand something for use in practical life, we must separate things.) Those who observe without prejudice will find that the play activity of a child until the age of seven has an individual character. As a player, the child is, in a certain sense, a kind of hermit. The child plays for itself alone. Certainly children want some help, but they are terribly egotistical and want the help only for themselves. With the change of teeth, play takes on a more social aspect. With some individual exceptions, children now want to play more with one another. The child ceases to be a hermit in his play; he wants to play with other children and to be something in play. . .but often the boys like to play soldier, (they at least want to be a general) and thus a social element is introduced to the children's play. . .

What occurs as the social element in play from the change of teeth until puberty is a preparation for the next period of life. In this next period, with the completion of puberty, independent reasoning arises. At that time human beings no longer subject themselves to authority; they form their own judgments and confront others as individuals. This same element appears in the previous period of life in play; it appears in something that is not connected with external social life, but in play. What occurs in the previous period of life, namely, social play, is the prelude to tearing yourself away from authority. We can therefore conclude that children's play until the age of seven actually enters the body only at the age of twenty-one or twenty-two, when we gain independence in our understanding and ability to judge experiences. On the other hand, what is prepared through play between the ages of seven and puberty appears at an earlier developmental stage in life, namely, during the period from puberty until about the age of twenty-one. This is a direct continuation. It is very interesting to notice that we have properly guided play during our first childhood years to thank for the capacities that we later have for understanding and experiencing life. In contrast, for what appears during our lazy or rebellious years we can thank the period from the change of teeth until puberty; thus, the connections in the course of human overlap. These overlapping connections have a fundamental significance of which psychology is unaware.

01/13/1921; in *Rudolf Steiner in the Waldorf School* [10], pp. 72-73

To be sure, the most important time with regard to people finding their way into life is not their school years, but a much later time, the time when they are in their twenties, between the ages of twenty and thirty. This is the time that earlier ages (which we cannot and do not want to wish back) called the transition from apprenticeship to mastery. There is sometimes something extremely sensible in the designation of such transitions.

This is the time in which people actually fully grow up. They must then find a way to become skillful in life. Then something happens that I would like to compare to the following image taken from nature. Let me remind you of a certain river that flows through Corinthia and Krain. As it flows from its source, it is known as the Poik. Then it disappears into a hole and is no longer visible. After a time it comes to the surface again. It is the same river; it has simply flowed underground for a while, but now as it continues above ground, it is called the Unz. Then it again disappears and flows underground. When it surfaces again, it is known as the Laibach. It surfaces again and again; it is the same water, but sometimes it flows underground.

It is also like this in a human life. There is something present in human life in the second, third, fourth, fifth, sixth, and seventh years of life, and also during the school years, in the form of children's urge to play. Everything that belongs to children's play is especially active at this age. Then, like the river, it sinks below the surface of human life. Later, when sexual maturity arrives and other things happen, we see that this urge to play is no longer active in the same way. But when people enter their twenties, the same thing that was present in play surfaces again. However, it no longer functions as the urge to play; it is now something different. It has now become the way in which the individual can find his or her way into life. And in fact, if children are allowed to play in the right way according to their particular potentials, when they are introduced to the right games, then they will be able to adapt to life in the right way. But if we miss out on something about the nature of the child in the games we introduce, the children will also lack skill in finding their place in life. This is how these things are related: The urge to play, the particular way in which a child plays, disappears and sinks below the surface of life. Then it resurfaces, but as something different, as the skill to adapt to life. There is an inner coherence in life throughout all its stages. We need to know this in order to teach children in the right way.

12/29/1920; in *The Spirit of the Waldorf School* [9]. Translated by JKS.

When one appreciates how the child plays in the first years of its life, up to about age five, one will accommodate the play of the child accordingly. Working with the intrinsic character of the child's individuality will prepare something in the child which will only come out much later in life. In order to do that, one has to be able to take the full span of human life into account. A botanist will observe the totality of the plant. Present day psychology tends to only look at an isolated moment in time. Let us observe the human being around age twenty-five to twenty-eight, or a little earlier, focusing on the time of life when we find our way into real life experience and should come to terms with the practicalities of life, the time when we gather real life experience and are becoming conscious of our aims. Adequate and exact observation of this phase of life will show how this is linked to the play of the child, between birth and age five more or less. The individual nature of play is a prelude to the way in which a person will meet life between age twenty and thirty; it will show in the way a person adapts and finds his aims in life. In early childhood we develop the roots, if I may express it this way, of what will appear later on as blossom. This type of insights can only be gained through perceiving interconnections in the way that anthroposophy can do by looking deeper into human nature. Such connections can only be perceived by taking the whole human being into account. We have to feel the total burden of the human being pressing on us so to speak, if we want to be proper educators. We have to feel how we can learn to perceive the particular predispositions to be found in every individual child.

02/24/1921; from an unpublished lecture held in Utrecht [25]. Translated by JKS.

But we also know that the child imitates when playing. Basically the urge to play is not totally original; things that the child perceives in the environment are imitated. The unprejudiced observer will observe soon enough that imitation lies at the basis of play. But every child plays differently. When one educates the little child before the age of seven, one must discern very carefully. In order to assess children's play properly, one needs an artistic sense, because things are different with every child. The early childhood educator must school his or her observation in order to develop an artistic eye to detect the individual quality of a child's play. In essence, each child's play is particular to that child.

The way a child plays, especially at ages four, five and six, goes down in a certain way into the depths of the soul as a force. The child grows up, and at first one does not notice anything about the way a particular way of playing comes out in later character traits. The child will develop other strengths and talents; what constituted the special character of the child's play goes down as it were into the hidden recesses of the soul. But later it reemerges in a particular way. It comes back between age twenty-five and thirty, which is the time of life in which we must find our way into the world; it is also the time of meeting the outer world and learning from experience and destiny. Some will fit in readily, others less readily. Some derive a certain satisfaction from their dealings with the world; others are less successful in what they undertake, they have a difficult destiny.

It is necessary to gain an overview of the totality of human life and see how the sense of play reemerges again in this sense of life between the ages of twenty-five and thirty. In that way one will get a picture that is artistic in nature, and one will know how to guide and direct the impulse to play in such a way that it will make a difference. It will give the child something for much later in life.

03/25/1923, "Education and Art"; in *Waldorf Education and Anthroposophy 2* [14], pp. 57-59

The high esteem for what is human and an extraordinary love for the human being are needed during one's evolving childhood days; this was the case for Schiller, whose (alas!) insufficiently known *Letters on the Esthetic Education of the Human Being* was based on those qualities.[4] We find in them a genuine appreciation of the artistic element in education, rooted in German culture. We can begin with these letters, and spiritual science will deepen our understanding. Look, for example, at child's play and how it flows forth simply because it is in a child's nature to be active. See how children liberate from their organization something that takes the form of play; their humanity consists of something that takes the form of play. Observe how necessity forces us to perform work that does not flow directly from the wholeness of our human nature; it can never express all of our nature. This is how we can begin to understand human development from childhood to adulthood.

There is one thing, however, that we should never lose sight of; usually, when observing children at play, people do so from the perspective of an adult. If this were not so, one would not hear again and again the trifling exhortation that "children should learn through play." The worst thing you could do is teach children that work is mere play, because when they grow up, they then will look at life as if it were only a game. Anyone who holds such a view must have observed children at play only with an adult's eyes, believing that children bring the same attitude to play as adults do. Play is fun for an adult, an enjoyment, a pleasure, the spice of life. But for children, play is the very stuff of life. Children are absolutely earnest about play, and the very seriousness of their play is a salient feature of

---

4 Johann Christoph Friedrich von Schiller (1759-1805), German poet, playwright, and critic.

this activity. Only by realizing the earnest nature of child's play can we understand this activity properly. And by watching how, in play, human nature pours itself in complete seriousness into the treatment of external objects, we can direct the child's inborn energy, capacity and gift for play into artistic channels. These still permit a freedom of inner activity while at the same time forcing children to struggle with outer materials, as we have to do in adult work. Then we can see how precisely this artistic activity makes it possible to conduct education so that the joy of engaging in artistic activities can be combined with the seriousness of play, contributing in this way to the child's character.

03/25/1923; in *Waldorf Education and Anthroposophy 2* [14], pp. 56-57

All children play. They do so naturally. Adults, on the other hand, have to work to live. They find themselves in a situation that demands it. If we look at social life today, we could characterize the difference between the child at play and the adult at work in the following way: Compared to the activities of the adult, which are dictated by necessity, the child's play is connected with an inner force of liberation, endowing the playing child with a feeling of well-being and happiness. You need only observe children at play. It is inconceivable that they are not in full inner accord with what they are doing. Why not? Because playing is a liberating experience to children, making them eager to release this activity from the organism. Freeing, joyful, and eager to be released, this is the character of the child's play.

What about the adult's work? Why does it often, if not usually, become an oppressive burden? (And this will be even more so in the future.) We could say that the child grows from an experience of liberation while playing into the experience of the oppressive burden of work, dictated to the adult by social conditions. Doesn't this great contrast beg us to ask: How can we build a bridge from the child's liberating play activity to the burdensome experience in the sphere of the adult workday?

If we follow the child's development with the artistic understanding I spoke of just now, we will find such a bridge in the role art plays at school. If applied properly as an educational tool, art will lead from the child's liberating play activity to the stage of adult work. With the help of art, this work no longer needs be an oppressive burden.

Unless we can divest work of its oppressive character, we can never solve the social question. Unless the polarity between the young child's playing and the adult's burdensome daily work is balanced by the right education, the problem of labor will reappear again and again in different guises.

04/14/1924; in *The Roots of Education* [19], p. 33

We need an art of teaching based on knowledge of human beings—knowledge of the child. This art of education will arise when we find a doctor's thesis that works with a case of diabetes at the age of forty by tracing it back to the harmful effects of the wrong kind of play in the third or fourth year. People will see then what we mean by saying that the human being consists of body, soul, and spirit, and that in the child, body, soul, and spirit are still a unity. The spirit and soul later become freed of the body, and a trinity is formed. In the adult, body, soul, and spirit are pushed apart, as it were, and only the body retains what the individual absorbed during early development as the seed of later life.

Now this is the strange thing: when an experience affects the soul, its consequences are soon visible, even when the experience was unconscious. Physical consequences, however, take seven or eight times longer to manifest. If you educate a child of three or four so that you present what will influence the soul's life, then the effect of this will appear in the eighth year; and people are usually careful to avoid doing anything with a child of four or five that may affect the soul life in an unhealthy way during the eighth or ninth year. Effects on the physical body take much longer to manifest, because the physical body must free itself of the soul and spirit. Therefore, something that influences the soul life at four or five may come to fruition in the physical body when that person is seven or eight times as old, for example, in the thirty-fifth year. Thus, a person may develop an illness during the late thirties or early forties caused by ill influences that affected that soul while at play as a child of three or four.

08/24/1922; in *The Spiritual Ground of Education* [15], p. 106

Thus it is necessary, for example, that teachers see precisely all that takes place when a small child plays. Play involves a whole constellation of soul activities: joy, sometimes pain, sympathy, antipathy, and especially curiosity and a desire for knowledge. Children want to investigate the objects they play with and see what they are made of. When we observe this free and entirely spontaneous expression of soul—still unconstrained into any form of work—we must look at the shades of feeling and whether it is satisfying. When we guide children's play toward contentment, we improve their health by promoting an activity that is indirectly connected with the digestive system. And the way a person's play is guided during childhood can determine whether a person's blood circulation and digestive system become congested in old age. There is a delicate connection between the way a child plays and the growth and development of the physical organism.

04/14/1924; in *The Roots of Education* [19]. Translated by JKS.

And what flows through us as teachers and educators into the children during the first phase of life works down into blood, breathing and digestion. It becomes a seed that grows into health or sickness some time around age forty or fifty. Yes, it is so: the way the educator behaves towards the young child forms the predisposition to inner happiness or unhappiness, to health or sickness.

01/06/1922, "Physical Education"; in *Soul Economy* [13], p. 264

In an education based on knowledge of the human being, the first step in this direction is to learn the particular ways children want to move when given freedom. Typical games with their inhibiting rules are quite alien to the nature of young children, because they suppress what should remain freely mobile in children. Organized games gradually dull their inner activity, and children lose interest in such externally imposed movements. We can clearly see this by observing what happens when the free movements of playing children are channeled too much into fixed gymnastic exercises. . .

Yet it is exactly this free play that we should observe and study. One must get to know children intimately, and then one sees what to do to stimulate the right kind of free play, in which boys and girls should, of course, participate together.

06/14/1920; in *Faculty Meetings with Rudolf Steiner, Volume One* [11], p. 95

A teacher: Should the preschool be like a kindergarten?

Dr. Steiner: The children have not started school yet. We cannot begin teaching them any subjects. You should occupy them with play. Certainly, they should play games. You can also tell stories in such a way that you are not teaching. But, definitely do not make any scholastic demands. Don't expect them to be able to retell everything. I don't think there is any need for an actual teaching goal there. We need to try to determine how we can best occupy the children. A teaching goal is not necessary. What you would do is play games, tell stories, and solve little riddles.

I would also not pedantically limit things. I would keep the children there until the parents pick them up. If possible, we could have them the whole day. If that is possible, then why not? You could also try some eurythmy with them, but don't spoil them. They shouldn't be spoiled by anything else, either. As I said, the main thing is that you mother the children. Don't be frivolous with them. You would not want to do anything academic with them. You can essentially do what you want.

In playing, the children show the same form as they will when they find their way into life. Children who play slowly will also be slow at the age of twenty and think slowly about all their experiences. Children who are superficial in play will also be superficial later. Children who say that they want to break open their toys to see what they look like inside will later become philosophers. That is the kind of thinking that overcomes the problems of life. In play, you can certainly do very much. You can urge a child who tends to play slowly, to play more quickly. You simply give the child games where some quickness is necessary.

Toys and Play Materials

When Rudolf Steiner talked about the pedagogy for the first seven years, he especially mentioned toys and play materials in connection with the development of the imagination of the child. He placed great value on very simple dolls and often took a big handkerchief out of his pocket while he was speaking in a lecture, tied a few knots in it and thus created something that was stimulating for the imagination. Numerous passages are quoted here which stress the importance of the doll. A few of these have already been quoted before in the passages concerning play, because it was difficult to take them out of context.

In addition Steiner recommends movable toys made out of wood, for example two hammering blacksmiths, and talks about the importance of books with movable pictures. He often has negative things to say about sets of building blocks and the like. Individual quotes were grouped together thematically to the extent that that was possible. Of course this wasn't possible in cases where Rudolf Steiner mentioned several types of toys in one passage.

The Doll

p. 52   Stimulation of the imagination by means of the primitive doll (1907 [2])

p. 52   Now the child's imagination is stimulated so it can be creative instead of having to put up with fixed, finished forms and contours. (12/29/1921 [13])

p. 54   Children inwardly abused by the "beautiful" doll. When the child looks at a handkerchief doll, formative forces are generated, shaping the brain's structure from out of the rhythmical system. (08/10/1923 [17])

p. 56   When playing with the primitive doll, the child springs to life each time and remains vitally engaged. (04/14/1924 [19])

p. 57   The primitive doll awakens the imagination; the inner organs begin to work. (12/01/1906 [3])

p. 57   Effect of the doll on the physical constitution of the child; making a doll with the child. (11/20/1922 [22])

p. 58   First the child is entirely a sense organ, and develops imagination through play, up to the time of the change of teeth; the materialistic age sins against this. The "beautiful" doll. (08/13/1924 [21])

p. 58   The atmosphere we create around the child is important; the effect of the "beautiful" doll. (03/03/1906 [24])

p. 59   The inner life of the child wilts next to the "beautiful" doll. (08/23/1922 [15])

p. 60   The inner forces are prevented from developing and working; calling forth the activity of the senses and stimulating them to become active. (08/27/1906 [6])

p. 60   Let them do sensible things with plain and simple objects; handkerchief doll. (06/12/1920 [11])

p. 60   A proper human imagination cannot be built up out of play with monkeys and bears. (07/19/1924 [20])

Movable Wooden Toys

p. 52   Two blacksmiths facing each other on movable wooden bases, hammering an object. (1907 [2])

Moving Picture Books

p. 52   Things that call forth a feeling of inner vitality are always better, for example, a moving picture book. (12/29/1921 [13])

p. 61   See chapter 1 of *The Course of My Life*. [1]

p. 61   From *Faculty Meetings with Rudolf Steiner*. (11/22/1920 [11])

p. 62   From a discussion with English guests in Dornach on 1/5/1922, quoted in *Kunst und Handarbeit* (Art and Handwork) by Hedwig Hauck.

p. 62   Answer to a question (12/29/1920 [9])

Sets of Building Blocks

Building blocks are discussed in the following quotes:

p. 52   (12/29/1921 [13])

p. 57   (12/01/1906 [3])

p. 62   (06/14/1920 [11])

p. 62   (12/29/1920 [9])

1907, in *The Education of the Child* [2], pp. 19-20

As the muscles of the hand grow firm and strong through doing the work for which they are suited, so the brain and other organs of the physical body of human beings are guided into the correct course of development if they receive the proper impressions from their environment. An example will best illustrate this point. You can make a doll for a child by folding up an old napkin, making two corners into legs, the other two corners into arms, a knot for the head, and painting eyes, nose and mouth with spot of ink. Or you can buy the child what is called a "pretty" doll, with real hair and painted cheeks. We need not dwell on the fact that the "pretty" doll is of course hideous and apt to spoil the healthy aesthetic sense for a lifetime; for education, the main question is different. If the children have the folded napkin before them, they have to fill in from their own imagination what is necessary to make it real and human. This work of the imagination shapes and builds the forms of the brain. The brain unfolds as the muscles of the hand unfold when they do the work they are suited for. By giving the child the so-called "pretty" doll, the brain has nothing more to do. Instead of unfolding, it becomes stunted and dried up.

If people could look into the brain as a spiritual investigator can, and see how it builds its forms, they would certainly give their children only play materials that stimulate and enliven its formative activity. Toys with dead mathematical forms alone have a desolating and killing effect on the formative forces of children; on the other hand whatever kindles the imagination of living things works in the proper way. Our materialistic age produces few good toys. It is certainly a healthy toy, for example, that, with movable wooden figures, represents two blacksmiths facing each other and hammering an anvil. These things can still be bought in rural areas. The picture books where the figures can be moved by pulling threads from below are also excellent and allow children themselves to transform a dead picture into a representation of living action. All of this causes a living mobility of the organs, and through such mobility the proper forms of the organs are built up.

12/29/1921, "Children Before the Seventh Year"; in *Soul Economy* [13], pp. 113-115

Whatever one's attitude may be, as educators we must respond to the imagination and fantasy of children, which tries to express itself outwardly when they play with toys or join in games with other children. The urge to play between the ages of two-and-a-half and five is really just the externalized activity of a child's power of fantasy. And if we have the necessary ability of observation for such matters, we can foretell a great deal about the future soul life of children merely by watching them play. The way young children play provides a clear indication of their potential gifts and faculties in later life. The most important thing now is to meet their inborn urge to play with the right toys. People in the past responded to this need according to their own particular understanding.

Perhaps this also happened in the West, but at one time a regular epidemic spread throughout Central Europe of giving children boxes of building bricks, especially at Christmas. From separate cubic and quadrilateral stones, children were expected to build miniature architectural monstrosities. This sort of thing has a far-reaching effect on the development of imagination in children, since it leads to an atomistic, materialistic attitude—a mentality that always wants to put bits and pieces together to form a whole. In dealing with practical life, it is far better to give full freedom to children's flexible and living powers of imagination than to nurture intellectual capacities that, in turn, encourage the atomistic nature of modern thinking. Imagination in children represents the very forces that have just liberated themselves from performing similar creative work within the physical formation of the brain. This is why we must avoid, as much as possible, forcing these powers of imagination into rigid, finished forms.

Imagine two nurses who are looking after a child between two and a half and five years of age. One of them—she may be very fond of the little girl in her charge—gives her a "beautiful" doll, one that has not only painted cheeks and real hair but eyes that close and a moveable head. I believe there are dolls that can even speak. Well, she gives this doll to the little girl, but since it is finished in every detail, there is nothing left for the child's imagination to create, and her yearning for creative flexibility remains unsatisfied. It is as if its forces of imagination were put into a straitjacket. The other nurse, who has a little more understanding for the inner needs of the child, takes an old piece of cloth that is of no use for anything else. She winds a thread around its upper end until something resembling a head appears. She may even ask the little girl to paint two black dots on the face or perhaps more, for the eyes, nose, and mouth.

Now, because the child's imagination is stimulated, because she can create instead of having to put up with fixed and finished forms, the child experiences a far more lively and intimate response than she does toward the so-called beautiful doll. Toys, as much as possible, should leave the power of fantasy free in children. And since intellect is not the same as fantasy or imagination, the activity of assembling many parts is really not in harmony with the type of fantasy that is characteristic of children at this age.

Anything that evokes an inner feeling of liveliness and flexibility is always suitable for young children. For example, there are children's books with cut-outs and nicely colored figures that can be moved by pulling strings attached below, so they will do all kinds of things, such as embracing or thrashing each other. These always stimulate children to invent whole stories, and thus they are very wholesome objects of play. Similarly, games with other children should not be too formal but should leave plenty of scope for children's imagination.

All these suggestions spring from a knowledge of the human being, based on reality and allowing educators to acquire the necessary understanding, especially in terms of the practical side of life.

08/10/1923, in *A Modern Art of Education* [17]

In this age too, when all eyes are so concentrated on the physical and external and there is so little understanding for the soul and spirit, a terrible form of punishment has crept in, a way of beating the child which is never realized as such, because men's minds are too little directed to the spirit.

Parents often think it desirable to give their little girl a "beautiful" doll as a plaything. This "beautiful" doll is a fearful production, because, for one thing, it is so utterly inartistic, in spite of its "real" hair, painted cheeks and eyes that close when it is laid down or lifted up! We often give our children toys that are dreadfully inartistic so-called copies of life: the doll is merely one example. All modern toys are tending to be of the same type, and they represent a form of cruel punishment to the child's inner nature. Even when punished children often behave well in the presence of others simply because convention demands it; equally out of politeness they do not always express aversion towards toys like the "beautiful" doll, although this dislike is deeply rooted in their souls. However strongly we may suggest to children that they ought to love such toys, the forces of their unconscious and subconscious life are stronger, and they have an intense antipathy to anything resembling the "beautiful" doll. For, as I will now show you, such toys really amount to an inner punishment.

Suppose that in the making of our playthings we were to take into consideration what the child has actually experienced in his young thought up to the age of six or seven, in the process of learning to stand upright and to walk, and then we were to make a doll out of a handkerchief, for instance, showing a head at the top with two ink-spots for eyes. The child can understand and, moreover, really love such a doll. Primitively, this doll possesses all the qualities of the human form, in so far as the child is capable of observing them at this early age. A child knows no more about the human being than that he stands upright, that there is an "upper" and a "lower" part of his being, that he has a head and a pair of eyes. As for the mouth, you will often find it on the forehead in a child's drawings! There is as yet no clear consciousness of the exact position of the mouth. What a child actually experiences is all contained in a doll made from a handkerchief with a couple of ink-spots for eyes. An inner, plastic force is at work in the child. All that comes to him from the environment passes over into his being and there becomes an inner formative power, a power that also builds up the organs of the body . . .

. . .If the child, for example, has a father who is constantly ill tempered and irritable, and as a result of this the child lives in an environment of perpetual shocks and unreasonableness, all this turmoil expresses itself in his breathing and the circulation of the blood. This means, however, that the lungs, heart, and the whole vascular system are affected by such a condition. Through the whole of his life the child bears, plastically formed within him, the inner effects of seeing his father's ill temper.

This is merely an example to show you that the child possesses a wonderful plastic power and is perpetually at work as a kind of inner sculptor upon his own being. If we give the child the kind of doll made from a handkerchief, these plastic, creative forces that arise in the human organism, especially from the rhythmic system of the breathing and blood circulation, and build up in the brain, flow gently upwards to the brain. They mold the brain like a sculptor who works upon his material with a fine and supple hand, a hand permeated with the forces of the soul and spirit. Everything here is in a formative process, in organic development. The child looks at the handkerchief-doll and that becomes formative force, real formative force, which then flows upwards from the rhythmic system and works upon the structure of the brain.

If, on the contrary, we give the child one of the so-called "beautiful" dolls which can move, which has moving eyes and painted cheeks, real hair, and so on, a hideous, ghostly production from the artistic point of view, then the plastic, brainbuilding forces that are generated in the rhythmic system have the effect of constant lashes of a whip. The child cannot as yet understand these things and it is as though the brain were enduring the lashings of a whip. The brain is thoroughly whipped, thoroughly flogged in a fearful way. Such is the secret of the "beautiful" doll and it can be applied to many of the playthings given to the child today.

04/14/1924, in *The Roots of Education* [19], pp. 31-32

We thus have to learn gradually that it is not so much a question of *inventing* from our own abstract thoughts all kinds of things for little children to do, such as using rods and so on. Children do not spontaneously do things like that. Their own soul forces must be aroused, and then they will imitate what the adults do. A little girl plays with a doll because she sees her mother nursing the baby. Whatever we see in adults is present in children as their tendency to imitate. This tendency must be considered in educating children up to the seventh year.

We must bear in mind, however, that what we educate is subject to change in the child's organism; in children everything is done in a more living and animated way than in adults, because children are still a unity of body, soul, and spirit. In adults, the body has been freed from the soul and spirit, and the soul and spirit from the body. Body, soul, and spirit exist side by side as individual entities; in the child they are still firmly united. This unity even penetrates the thinking.

We can see these things very clearly through an example. A small child is often given a so-called "beautiful" doll, a painted creature with glass eyes, made to look exactly like a human being. These little horrors are made to open and shut their eyes and do all sorts of other things. These are then presented to children as "beautiful" dolls. Even from an artistic perspective they are hideous; but I will not enlarge on that now. But consider what really happens to a child who is presented with a doll of this kind, a doll that can open its eyes and so on. At first the child will love it because it is a novelty, but that does not last.

Now, compare that with what happens to a child if I just take a piece of rag and make a doll out of that. Tie it together for a head, make two dots for eyes, and perhaps a big nose, and there you have it. Give that to a child and she will fill out the rest through imagination in soul and spirit, which are so closely connected with the body. Then, every time that child plays with the doll, there is an inner awakening that remains inwardly active and alive. By making such experiments yourself, you will see what a difference there is between giving a child playthings that leave as much as possible to the power of imagination and giving finished toys that leave nothing for the child's own inner activity.

12/01/1906, in *The Education of the Child* [3], p. 57

So you can see that spiritual investigation sheds light even on practical details. The developing organs must be treated in ways that promote their health and inner forces. The child should not be given toys that are too finished and perfect, such as building blocks or perfect dolls. A doll made out of an old table napkin on which eyes, nose and mouth are indicated is far better. Any child will see such a homemade doll as a lady attired in beautiful finery. Why? Because it stirs the imagination, and that induces movement in the inner organs, and it produces a feeling of well being in the child. Notice how such a child plays in a lively and interested way, throwing body and soul into what the imagination conjures up, while the child with the perfect doll just sits, unexcited and unamused. It has no possibility to add anything through imagination, so the inner organs are condemned to inactivity. Children have an extraordinarily sound instinct for what is good for them, as long as only the physical body has become free to interact with the external world, and as long as they are in the process of development.

11/20/1922, in GA 218 [22]. Translated by JKS.

Up to the change of teeth, we could say, the child will be surrounded by the world of parents and family. But in addition to that, children's schools will be needed, schools for playing. We only do the right thing by the child when we know how the play of the young child works on in the physical organism; then we can act accordingly in how we develop the activity of play. Just imagine how it is for a child to get a ready-made doll, for example, one of those "beautiful" dolls, complete with a beautifully painted face, one that is, in other words, as "perfect" as it can be, imagine what that does for a child. Coarse anatomy won't reveal these things, but such a child's blood-flow will be tardy, and the physical organization will be disturbed. We are completely unaware of what a grave sin we are committing there, how such dolls works on the child! When, on the other hand, we put together a doll ourselves from some rags, when we do this together with a child, and when we paint eyes on the cloth so that the child witnesses this as it is being done, in the moment of creation, then this will be absorbed into his or her organism and mobilize it; it will go into the blood and the breathing.

08/13/1924, in *The Kingdom of Childhood* [21], pp. 21-22

You should experience the changing of the teeth through careful observation like this. The fact that children were previously wholly sense organ now enables them to develop above all the gift of fantasy and symbolism. And you must take this into consideration even in play. Our materialistic age sins terribly against this. Take, for example, the so-called "beautiful" doll that are so often given to children these days. They have such beautifully formed faces, wonderfully painted cheeks, and even eyes with which they can go to sleep when laid down, real hair and goodness knows what all! But this kills the fantasy of the child, for it leaves nothing to the imagination and the child can take no great pleasure in it. But if you make a doll out of a napkin or a handkerchief with two ink spots for eyes, a dab of ink for a mouth, and some sort of arms, then with imagination that child can add a great deal to it.

It is particularly good for children to be given the opportunity to add as much as possible to playthings out of their own fantasy. This enables children to develop a symbolizing activity. Children should have as few things as possible that are finished and complete and what people call "beautiful." For the beauty of such a doll that I have described above with real hair and so on, is only a conventional beauty. In truth it is ugly because it is so inartistic.

03/03/1906 [24]. Translated by JKS.

What matters are the thoughts, the attitude and the atmosphere with which one surrounds the child. . .It depends on the surroundings how the attitude of the child in turn will take shape in a noble direction or not. It is therefore possible to influence the child, systematically, fully consciously, by setting an example in ordinary, daily life. Everything children absorb goes in through the senses, and children will imitate everything that goes in. In this way one is able to influence the child harmoniously.

It would be a very important thing to work with this thought in anthroposophical circles, in order to perceive better and better how incredibly important the surroundings are for a small child. Let us try to clarify this in more detail. Many people believe they do a child a great favor with a "beautiful" doll. In the eyes of a clairvoyant, however, this is the worst thing one can do for a child. By giving a child a "beautiful" doll one forces the child's urge to imitate into prescribed channels rather than stimulating it; the creative power is killed. When one observes children rightly, one will see more often than not that they throw the most beautiful toys away and make new ones out of the simplest materials. Imitation should not curtail the imagination. Children have to live in an imaginative world; they should be occupied by playing and pretending and thus develop their own forces in creating their own world of inner pictures. And a "beautiful" doll will not activate this inner force. What children play is done in imitation of what they hear and see; playing demands exercise of the will. This awakens certain energies, and two things will be fostered: dexterity and the ability to maintain equanimity in the face of a great diversity of circumstances. These are a few starting points from which to view the education of the small child.

08/23/1922, in *The Spiritual Ground of Education* [15], p. 98

May I say something very heretical? People are very fond of giving dolls to children, especially pretty dolls. They fail to see that children really don't want this. They wave it away, but it is forced on them—pretty dolls, all painted. It is far better to give children a handkerchief, or, if you can't spare that, a piece of cloth. You tie it together, make the head here, paint the nose, two eyes, and so on. [Steiner demonstrates with his own handkerchief.] Healthy children much prefer to play with these than with the pretty dolls, because something is left to the imagination. The most magnificent doll with red cheeks and such leaves nothing for the imagination to do. The fine doll brings an inner emptiness to a child.

08/27/1906, in *At the Gates of Spiritual Science* [6]

The most important thing during the first seven years is to nourish a child's sense organs. He will see with his eyes how people round him are behaving. Hence, during these years we must try to influence a child's senses, to draw them out so that they become active on their own account. That is why it is such a mistake to give a child one of those "beautiful" dolls. They hinder him from setting his own inner powers to work. A normal child will reject the doll and be much happier with a piece of wood, or with anything that gives his imagination a chance to be active.

06/12/1920, in *Faculty Meetings with Rudolf Steiner* [11], p. 80

You can probably work best with the children you have when you have them do meaningful things with simple objects. Anything! You should try to discover what interests the children. There are children, particularly girls, who can make a doll out of any handkerchief. The dolls write letters and then pass them on. You could be the postman or the post office. Do sensible things with simple objects.

When the change of teeth begins, the children enter the stage when they want to imagine things, for instance that one thing is a rabbit and another is a dog, sensible things that the child dreams into. The principle of play is that until the change of teeth, the child imitates sensible things, dolls and puppets. With boys, it is puppets, with girls, dolls. Perhaps they could have a large puppet with a small one alongside. These need only be a couple pieces of wood. At age seven, you can bring the children into a circle or ring, and they can imagine something. Two could be a house, and the others go around and live in it. In that game, the children are themselves.

With musical children, you can play something else, perhaps something that would support their musical talent. You should help unmusical children develop their musical capacities through dance and eurythmy. You need to be inventive. You can do all these things, but you need to be inventive, because otherwise everything becomes stereotyped. Later, it is easier because you can connect with things in the school.

07/19/1924, in *Human Values in Education* [20], pp. 60-61

. . . "beautiful" dolls, with real hair, with pretty faces, with eyes that close when the dolls are laid down, and so on. Modern society considers them beautiful, but they are hideous, because they show no artistic qualities. What sort of dolls are these? They are dolls that cannot activate a child's fantasy. Now let us try something different. Tie a handkerchief so that you have a figure with arms and legs; then make eyes with blobs of ink and perhaps a mouth with red ink as well; now a child must develop imagination to see the human form. This kind of thing works with tremendous living force on children, because it offers them the possibility of using fantasy.

Of course, we must do this ourselves first. But the possibility must be provided for children, and this must be done at the age when everything is play. This is why all the toys that do not stimulate fantasy in children are so damaging to them. As I said, today those "beautiful" dolls are somewhat outdated, because now we give monkeys or bears to children. Nor do such toys provide an opportunity for developing an imagination related to the human being. Suppose a child runs up to you, and you offer a bear for the child to cuddle. This sort of thing clearly shows how far our society is from being able to penetrate the depths of human nature.

From *Autobiography-Chapters in the Course of my Life* [1]. Translated by JKS.

I was captivated especially by certain kinds of toys that I still value highly today. They were picture books with movable figures, which could be pulled below the page with threads. One would follow along small stories with the help of these pictures, which one could bring to life oneself by pulling the threads. I would sit for hours on end with such picture books, together with my sister. From them I also learned the first basics of reading, and this seemed to happen by itself.

11/22/1920, in *Faculty Meetings with Rudolf Steiner* [11], p. 212

You have a system with the moveable pictures that have strings attached to them; you have a short text and above it a moveable picture.[5] I find that very useful for picture books. Such picture books are extremely necessary in kindergarten. If you would only continue to work on it! Modern books are so boring.

---

5 The idea was later taken up by Hilde Langen, who published several children's stories in that form.

From a discussion with English guests held on 1/5/1922 in Dornach, quoted in *Kunst und Handarbeit* (Art and Handwork), by Hedwig Hauck. Translated by JKS.

Question: How can educators best meet the needs of children from five-and-a-half to seven years old, who usually ask what they should do?

Dr. Steiner: Well, in children of that age the feeling for authority is already somewhat present, but the urge to imitate still has the upper hand. That should be the guiding principle for what one does with those children. What I indicated about the picture books with moveable figures applies especially to children of that age; those books work extremely well. It is a good thing to occupy their awakening life of imagination with those types of books.

06/14/1920, in *Faculty Meetings with Rudolf Steiner* [11], p. 99

It is certainly a correct observation that this poor handwriting first started when children's toys became so extraordinarily materialistic. It is terrible that such a large number of toys are construction sets. They really are not toys at all because they are atomistic. If a child has a simple worktable, then the child should learn to use it. I wish that children had toys that moved. This is all contained in *The Education of the Child*. The toys today are terrible, and for that reason the children learn no dexterity and write poorly.

12/29/1920, Answer to a question [9]. Translated by JKS.

. . . I would like to point out that one does not harm the individuality of the child when one does not pay too much attention to the types of games which combine separate elements. In fact, from the standpoint of spiritual science, one should consider those types of games less valuable. Erector sets, building blocks and the like appeal too strongly to the intellect of the child. Much more beneficial types of playthings are those which bring more life to the child and such toys will vary according to the individuality of the child. I have been trying for a long time to promote this—but it is hard to make people enthusiastic for such small matters, such seeming trivial things—to reintroduce picture books for children with movable figures. There used to be such picture books, which had figures that one could move with strings at the bottom of the page; the figures would move, and whole stories could be created with them. Suitably varied according to the needs of individual children, this can have a highly beneficial effect. By contrast, things that remain still and also games that appeal to combining elements such as building blocks, are in fact not suitable for children's play. Building blocks are, after all, only a result of the materialism of our time.

I would also like to point out that the main thing one has to assess in games is to what degree the imagination of the child is allowed to be active. You can destroy the most beautiful powers in a human being by giving a child, a growing, developing child, a "beautiful" clown (in the case of boys) or a very "beautiful" doll (in the case of girls) from an artistic point of view, they are always awful, but the people who design them strive to make them "beautiful" dolls. . .Play materials that leave the greatest possible room for a child's imagination are the best. The child feels basically most happy with a doll or clown made out of a handkerchief, tied together at the top to form a little head. Such things should be fostered. Basically, it should be possible to turn soul activity into life and mobility. One will definitely find the right thing when one has an eye for temperaments, for example by giving a highly excited child really the most complicated toys possible, and by giving a slow child the simplest toys. The same method should be applied when it comes work done by hand. What a child does out of her own inclination is also very important for later years. One should follow the inner inclination of the child in letting the child walk slowly or fast: one should let an excited child walk fast, and induce a slow child which is lazy in thinking, to walk slowly in games or at other occasions. So in adapting the play to the individual the point is to treat like with the like and not the opposite. Those who really strive to treat children appropriately in the way that is described will get very far with these directions.

Creating the Right Environment for the Child

From the quotations above it is clear how important it is that special attention is given to the way the surroundings of the child are created. In order to create a good working atmosphere, the outward aspects and care of the environment are important, but there is also the inner attitude of the early childhood educator. The latter is equally perceptible for the child. In the following quotations the effect of the environment on the developing child is expressed.

p. 67   The first physical surroundings after birth, from the etheric mother sheath until the seventh year of life. Joy in the surroundings. Nothing which may not be imitated should happen around the child. (1907 [2])

The influence of thoughts around the child:
p. 69   (08/10/1923 [17])
p. 69   (08/29/1924 [14])

p. 69   The child makes everything in his surroundings part of his own being. (03/26/1923 [14]).

p. 70   The child as a sense organ and the relationship to the surroundings. (08/29/1924 [14]).

p. 70   The child is a sense organ in which the will is at work. (04/19/1923 [16])

p. 70   The development of a healthy, strong will. (1907 [2])

p. 71   Impressions from the environment "ripple" through the
         organism of the child; one should not allow oneself any other
         thoughts in the company of the child than those which can
         continue to "vibrate" in the child. (1907 [2])
         (04/19/1924 [18])

p. 72   The effect of the surroundings on the inner physical makeup of
         the child. (08/30/1924 [14])

p. 72   Importance of the virtue of thankfulness around the child.
         (04/20/1923 [16])

With physical birth, the physical human body is exposed to the physical environment of the external world. Before birth, the protecting envelope of the mother's body surrounds it. What the forces and fluids of the enveloping mother's body have done for it thus far, must, from now on, be done by the forces and benevolence of the external physical world. Before the change of teeth in the seventh year, the human body has to accomplish a task on itself that is essentially different from the tasks of any other period of life. In this period the physical organs must form themselves into definite shapes; their whole structural nature must receive particular tendencies and directions. (Growth takes place in later periods as well; but throughout the whole succeeding life growth is based on the forces developed in this first life-period.) If true forms were developed, true forces would grow: if misshapen forms were developed, misshapen forms would grow. We can never repair what we have neglected as educators in the first seven years. Just as nature causes the proper environment for the physical human body before birth, so after birth the educator must provide for the proper physical environment. Only the right physical environment works on the child in such a way that the physical organs correctly shape themselves.

Two "magic" words indicate how children enter into relationship with their environment. These words are *imitation* and *example*. . . Children imitate what happens in their physical environment, and in this process of imitation their physical organs are cast in the forms that thus become permanent. "Physical environment" must, however, be understood in the widest sense imaginable. It includes not just what happens around children in the material sense, but everything that occurs in their environment, everything that can be perceived by their senses, that can work on the inner powers of children from the surrounding physical space. This includes all moral or immoral actions, all wise or foolish actions that children see.

It is not moralistic talk or wise admonitions that influence children in this sense, but it is, rather, what adults do visibly before their eyes. The effect of admonition is that it shapes the forms, not of the physical, but of the etheric body. The etheric body is surrounded until the seventh year by a protecting etheric envelope, even as the physical body is surrounded before physical birth by the physical envelope of the mother-body. Everything that must evolve in the etheric body before the seventh year, ideas, habits, memory, and so on, all of this must develop "by itself," just as the eyes and ears develop within the mother-body without the influence of external light. The information in Jean Paul's excellent educational work, *Levana* or *Science of Education*, is no doubt true. He says that travelers have learned more from their nurses in their first years of life than they will in all of their journeys around the world. Children, however, do not learn by instruction or admonition, but through imitation. The physical organs shape themselves through the influence of the physical environment. Good sight will be developed in children if their environment has the proper conditions of light and color, while in the brain and blood circulation the physical foundations will be laid for a healthy moral sense if children see moral actions in their environment. If, before their seventh year, children see only foolish actions in their surroundings, the brain will assume the forms that adapt it to foolishness in later life. . .

. . .The joy of children in and with their environment must therefore be counted among the forces that build and shape the physical organs. They need teachers that look and act with happiness and, most of all, with honest, unaffected love. Such a love that streams, as it were, with warmth through the physical environment of the children may be said to literally "hatch" the forms of the physical organs.

The children who live in such an atmosphere of love and warmth, and who have around them truly good examples to imitate, are living in their proper element. One should thus strictly guard against anything being done in the children's presence that they should not imitate. One should not do anything that one would then have to say to a child, "You should not do that." The strength of children's tendency to imitate can be recognized by observing how they paint and scribble written signs and letters long before they understand them. Indeed, it is good that they paint the letters first by imitation and only later learn to understand their meaning. For imitation belongs to the time when the physical body is developing, while meaning speaks to the etheric, and the etheric body should not be worked on until after the change of teeth, after the outer etheric envelope has fallen away. All learning associated with speech in these years should be especially through imitation. Children will best learn to speak through hearing; no rules or artificial instruction of any kind can be good for this.

It is important to realize the value of children's songs, for example, as a means of education in early childhood. They must make pretty and rhythmical impressions on the senses; the beauty of sound is of greater value than the meaning. The more alive the impression is on the eye and ear the better. Dancing movements in musical rhythm have a powerful influence in building up the physical organs, and this should also not be undervalued.

08/10/1923, *A Modern Art of Education* [17]

Now, because the child is a most delicately balanced organ of sense, he is not only sensitive to the physical influences of his surroundings, but also to the moral influences, especially those of thought. However far-fetched it may appear to the modern materialistic mind, the child does, nevertheless, sense all that those in his environment are thinking. As parents or teachers we must not only refrain from actions that are outwardly unseemly, we must be inwardly true, inwardly moral in our thought and feeling, for the child senses these things and absorbs them. He does not merely shape his nature according to our words and actions, but in accordance with our whole attitude of heart and mind. The environment, then, is the most important thing of all in the first period of the child's education up to the seventh year.

08/29/1924, "Educational Issues"; in *Waldorf Education and Anthroposophy 2* [14], pp. 196-97

The only principle necessary at this stage is that human behavior should be worthy of imitation. This includes also thinking, because in their own way, children perceive whether our thoughts are moral or not. People do not usually believe in these imponderables, but they are present nevertheless. While around young children, we should not allow ourselves even a single thought that is unworthy of being absorbed by the child.

03/26/1923, "Education and the Moral Life"; in *Waldorf Education and Anthroposophy 2* [14], p. 66

Until age seven, children are entirely given over to the influences coming from their environment. The following comparison can be made: I breathe in the oxygen of the air, which is part of my surroundings, to unite, at the next moment, my bodily nature with it, thus changing some part of the external world into my own inner world, where it works, lives, and weaves within me. Likewise, with each indrawn breath, children up to the age of seven bring outer influences into their "inner soul breath," by incorporating every gesture, facial expression, act, word, and even each thought coming from their surroundings. Just as the oxygen in my surroundings pulsates in my lungs, the instruments of my breathing, and blood circulation, so everything that is part of the surroundings pulsates through the young child.

08/29/1923, in *Waldorf Education and Anthroposophy 2* [14], p. 195

. . .(T)he young child is almost entirely one sense organ. What is the nature of a sense organ? It surrenders fully to the world. Consider the eye. The entire visible world is mirrored in the eye and is contained in it. The eye is totally surrendered to the world. Likewise the child, though in a different way, is surrendered fully to the environment. We adults may taste sweet, bitter, or acid tastes on the tongue and with the palate, but the tastes do not penetrate our entire organism. Although we are not usually aware of it, it is nevertheless true to say that when the baby drinks milk the taste of the milk is allowed to permeate the entire organism. The baby lives completely like an eye, like one large sense organ. The differentiation between outer and inner senses occurs only later.

04/19/1923, in *The Child's Changing Consciousness* [16], p. 99

Within this same context we must now look at another point. During the initial period of life, that is, from birth until the change of teeth, the child lives like one great multifaceted sense organ, but as a sense organ where will forces were working in every moment of life. For me to use the expression "a sense organ where will forces are working" may sound strange, but this is only because of the complete inadequacy of what we are told by contemporary physiology and the popular ideas derived from it. Today one does not associate will forces with the function of the human eye, for example. Nevertheless, even in the eye, the perceived image is due to will activity. The same is true of the functioning of every other sense organ: will substance is instrumental in creating the inner sense impressions. The task of a sense organ, first of all, is to expose itself, or the human being, passively to the external world's influences. But within every sense organ an inner activity also occurs that has a will nature.

1907, in *The Education of the Child* [2], pp. 33-34

By a proper application of fundamental educational principles during the first seven years of childhood, the foundation is laid for the development of a strong and healthy will; for a strong and healthy will must have its support in well-developed forms of the physical body.

1907, in *The Education of the Child* [2], pp. 20-21

. . .(D)uring the first period of life the child is in the highest degree and by its whole nature a being of sense. The child is like a sense organ. The surrounding impressions ripple, echo and sound through the whole organism because the child is not so inwardly bound up with its body as is the case in later life, but lives in the environment with its freer spiritual and soul nature. Hence the child is receptive to all the impressions coming from the environment.

04/09/1924, in *The Essentials of Education* [18], pp. 27-28

In other words, we need to become more aware of how anything acting as a stimulus in the environment continues to vibrate in the child. We must be very clear that, in this sense, we are dealing with imponderables.

Children are aware, whenever we do something in their environment, of the thoughts behind a hand-gesture or facial expression. Children intuit them: they do not, obviously, interpret facial features since what operates instead is a much more powerful inner connection between the child and adult than will exist later between adults. Consequently, we must never allow ourselves to feel or think anything around children that should not be allowed to ripple on within the child. The rule of thumb for all relationships in early education must be this. Whether in perception, feeling, or thought, whatever we do around children must be done in such a way that it may be allowed to continue vibrating their souls.

The psychologist, the observer of souls, the person of broad practical experience, and the doctor thus all become a unity, insofar as the child is concerned. This is important, since anything that makes an impression on the child, anything that causes the soul's response, continues in the blood circulation and digestion, becoming a part of the foundation of health in later years. Due to the imitative nature of the child, whenever we educate the spirit and soul of the child, we also educate the body and physical nature of the child. This is the wonderful metamorphosis—that whatever approaches children and touches their spirit and soul, becomes their physical, organic organization, and their predisposition to health or illness in later life.

08/30/1924, in *Waldorf Education and Anthroposophy 2* [14], p. 212

Our being, as adults, enters a child's being just as the candlelight enters the eye. Whatever we are around a child spreads its influence so that the child's blood circulates differently in the sense organs and in the nerves; since these operate differently in the muscles and vascular liquids that nourish them, the entire being of the child is transformed according to the external sense impressions received. One can notice the effect that the moral and religious environment of childhood has had on an old person, including the physical constitution. A child's future condition of health and illness depends on our ability to realize deeply enough that everything in the child's environment is mirrored in the child. The physical and moral elements are reflected and affect a person's health or illness later.

04/20/1923, in *The Child's Changing Consciousness* [16], pp. 125-128

And yet gratitude is a virtue that, in order to play a proper role in the human soul, must grow with the child. Gratitude is something that must already flow into the human being when the growth forces, working in the child in an inward direction, are liveliest, when they are at the peak of their shaping and molding activities. Gratitude is something that has to be developed out of the bodily-religious relationship I described as the dominant feature in the child from birth until the change of teeth. At the same time, however, gratitude will develop very spontaneously during this first period of life, as long as the child is treated properly. All that flows with devotion and love from a child's inner being toward whatever comes from the periphery through the parents or other educators, and everything expressed outwardly in the child's imitation, will be permeated with a natural mood of gratitude. We only have to act in ways that are worthy of the child's gratitude and it will flow toward us, especially during the first period of life. This gratitude then develops further by flowing into the forces of growth that make the limbs grow, and that alter even the chemical composition of the blood and other bodily fluids. This gratitude lives in the physical body and must dwell in it, since it would not otherwise be anchored deeply enough.

It would be very incorrect to remind children constantly to be thankful for whatever comes from their surroundings. On the contrary, an atmosphere of gratitude should grow naturally in children through merely witnessing the gratitude that their elders feel as they receive what is freely given by their fellow human beings, and in how they express their gratitude. In this situation, one would also cultivate the habit of feeling grateful by allowing the child to imitate what is done in the surroundings. If a child says "thank you" very naturally—not in response to the urging of others, but simply by imitation—something has been done that will greatly benefit the child's whole life. Out of this an all-embracing gratitude will develop toward the whole world.

The cultivation of this universal gratitude toward the world is of paramount importance. It does not always need to be in one's consciousness, but may simply live in the background of the feeling life, so that, at the end of a strenuous day, one can experience gratitude, for example, when entering a beautiful meadow full of flowers. Such a subconscious feeling of gratitude may arise in us whenever we look at nature. It may be felt every morning when the sun rises, when beholding any of nature's phenomena. And if we only act properly in front of the children, a corresponding increase in gratitude will develop within them for all that comes to them from the people living around them, from the way they speak or smile, or the way such people treat them.

This universal mood of gratitude is the basis for a truly religious attitude; for it is not always recognized that this universal sense of gratitude, provided it takes hold of the whole human being during the first period of life, will engender something even further. In human life, love flows into everything if only the proper conditions present themselves for development. The possibility of a more intense experience of love, reaching the physical level, is given only during the second period of life between the change of teeth and puberty. But that first tender love, so deeply embodied in the inner being of the child, without as yet working outward, this tender blossom will become firmly rooted through the development of gratitude. Love, born out of the experience of gratitude during the first period of the child's life, is the love of God. One should realize that, just as one has to dig the roots of a plant into the soil in order to receive its blossom later on, one also has to plant gratitude into the soul of the child, because it is the root of love of God. The love of God will develop out of universal gratitude, as the blossom develops from the root. . .If, during the first period of life, we create an atmosphere of gratitude around children. . .then out of this gratitude toward the world, toward the entire universe, and also out of a thankfulness for being in this world at all (which is something that should ensoul all people), the most deep-seated and warmest piety will grow. Not the kind that lives on one's lips or in thought only, but piety that will pervade the entire human being, which will be upright, honest, and true.

As for gratitude, it must grow; but this can happen with the intensity necessary for such a soul and spiritual quality only when it develops from the child's tender lifestirrings during the time from birth to its change of teeth. And then this gratitude will become the root of the love of God. It is the foundation for the love of God.

References

The quotations in this book are all taken from Rudolf Steiner's works. Each of these works has a standard number in the collected works of Rudolf Steiner, the Gesamtausgabe, published by Rudolf Steiner Verlag, Dornach, Switzerland. In the list of English titles below, the corresponding "GA number" is given. Where possible, the titles of the most recent translations are used. Throughout the text, reference is made to this list of twenty-six works through the numbers in brackets. Where page numbers are indicated in the text, the reference is to the particular English edition listed here.

[1] *Mein Lebensgang*, GA 28. *Autobiography—Chapters in the Course of My Life: 1861-1907.*

[2] *Luzifer-Gnosis*, GA 34. *The Education of the Child*, 1996 edition, Anthroposophic Press.

[3] *Die Erkenntnis des Übersinnlichen in unserer Zeit und deren Bedeutung fur das heutige Leben* (Berlin und Koln) GA 55, included in *The Education of the Child*, 1996 edition, Anthroposophic Press.

[4] *Antworten der Geisteswissenschaft auf die grossen Fragen des Daseins* (Berlin), GA 60, included in *The Education of the Child*, 1996 edition, Anthroposophic Press.

[5] *Menschengeschichte im Lichte der Geistesforschung* (Berlin) GA 61. *Self- Education: The Self-Development of Man in the Light of Anthroposophy.* (typescript)

[6] *Vor dem Tore der Theosophie* (Stuttgart), GA 95. *At the Gates of Spiritual Science.*

[7] *Die spirituellen Hintergruende der auesseren Welt. Der Sturz der Geister der Finsternis* (Dornach), GA 177. *The Fall of the Spirits of Darkness.*

[8] *Die Erziehungsfrage als soziale Frage* (Dornach), GA 296. *Education as a Force for Social Change,* 1997 edition, Anthroposophic Press.

[9] *Die Waldorfschule und ihr Geist* (Basel/Stuttgart/Dornach), GA 297. *The Spirit of the Waldorf School.*

[10] *Rudolf Steiner in der Waldorfschule* (Stuttgart), GA 298. *Rudolf Steiner in the Waldorf School,* 1996 edition, Anthroposophic Press.

[11] *Konferenzen (mit Rudolf Steiner),* GA 300. *Faculty Meetings with Rudolf Steiner, Vol. 1,* 1998 edition, Anthroposophic Press.

[12] *Die Erneuerung der paedagogisch-didaktischen Kunst durch Geisteswissenschaft,* (Basel), GA 301. *The Renewal of Education,* 2001 edition, Anthroposophic Press.

[13] *Die gesunde Entwicklung des Leiblich-Physischen als Grundlage der freien Entfaltung des Seelisch-Geistigen* (Dornach), GA 303. *Soul Economy: Body, Soul, and Spirit in Waldorf Education,* 2003 edition, Anthroposophic Press.

[14] *Anthroposophische Menschenkunde und Paedagogik (verschiedene Stadte),* GA 304a. *Waldorf Education and Anthroposophy 2,* 1996 edition, Anthroposophic Press.

[15] *Die geistig-seelischen Grundkraefte der Erziehungskunst* (Oxford), GA 305. *The Spiritual Ground of Education,* 2004 edition, Anthroposophic Press.

[16] *Die paedagogische Praxis yom Gesichtspunkte geisteswissenschaftlicher Menschenerkenntnis* (Dornach), GA 306. *The Child's Changing Consciousness,* 1996 edition, Anthroposophic Press.

[17] *Gegenwartiges Geistesleben und Erziehung* (Ilkley), GA 307. *A Modern Art of Education.*

[18] *Die Methodik des Lehrens und die Lebensbedingungen des Erziehens* (Stuttgart), GA 308. *The Essentials of Education,* 1997 edition, Anthroposophic Press.

[19] *Anthroposophische Pädagogik und ihre Voraussetzungen* (Bern), GA 309. *The Roots of Education,* 1997 edition, Anthroposophic Press.

[20] *Der paedagogische Wert der Menschenerkenntnis und der Kulturwert der Paedagogik* (Arnheim), GA 310. *Human Values in Education,* 2004 edition, Anthroposophic Press.

[21] *Die Kunst des Erziehens aus dem Erfassen der Menschenwesenheit,* GA 311. *The Kingdom of Childhood,* 1995 edition, Anthroposophic Press.

The following have not yet been translated:

[22] *Geistige Zusammenhaenge des menschlichen Organismus (verschiedene Stadte),* GA 218. The lecture of November 20, 1922 is not translated.

[23] *Der Weg zu Gesundem Denken und die Lebenslage des Gegenwartsmenschen,* GA 335, (*Die Erziehung und der Unterricht gegenueber der Weltlage der Gegenwart*).

[24] March 3, 1906, Hamburg.

[25] February 24, 1921, Utrecht.

[26] January 1, 1922, Dornach (discussion).

Playing, Learning, Meeting the Other

Preface
FROM THE 2006 GERMAN EDITION

At Easter-time in 2005 a large international conference of kindergarten teachers took place in Dornach at the Goetheanaum. More than 1000 people from around the world were able to participate. This booklet was prepared to fulfill the frequently-expressed wish that the collected lectures be published.

The theme of the conference arose from burning questions that can be heard all over the world. Free play of little children is in decline. The motto of "playful learning" is heard everywhere, especially since the onset of the Programme for International Student Assessment (PISA). Children play in learning games, in early musical education, in English courses, in gymnastics courses, in animation. But all these types of play are directed from outside, and do not come out of children's own inner activity. We wanted to focus carefully on the kind of play that promotes health and is freeing, play by means of which the child educates herself, and learns as much as she can actually handle. This brought us to the theme of play that is tied to learning, to acceleration.

The problem, however, does not originate in the children. We as adults often meet the child in such a way that pressure to perform, stress, confusion, and illness are the result. Then we have to deal with "difficult" children. So the theme of meeting the other definitely fits in with this.

We live in a time in which it is incumbent upon us to individually school ourselves to meet children, parents and colleagues. Since we are living in the time of the consciousness soul, we seek meetings that do not remain on the surface, but go deeper and can be sensed by the powers of the heart. The conference was meant to instill the courage needed to go out as Waldorf educators and fight for the real needs of children.

The following passages from Rudolf Steiner's works form the basis for the theme:

1907, in *The Education of the Child*

Free space is given for the human being to develop; space to play. This is also the best way to meet the child. It is best if we do not give children fixed concepts, ideas of the kind which are bound in fixed contours, but ideas which are such that they give thoughts room to play, that these thoughts can go this way or that way. Only in such a way will one succeed in having thoughts find the course which is prescribed by the inner disposition of the child.

1924, in *Waldorf Education and Anthroposophy 2*

It is like this: people look at children's play from the point of view of grown-ups. Were this not the case, we would never hear the dilettante phrase that children in school should "learn as effortlessly as in a game," as is repeated so often. You could do nothing worse than that, actually. If we would achieve that, our only accomplishment would be that the children would make a game out of life when grown-up.

1921, in *Soul Economy and Waldorf Education*

We [must] learn to understand the way in which the child wants to be freely active in play. Everything we bring to the child in the way of stereotypical or contrived forms of play will saddle the child up with something which is foreign to his nature and will suppress what should be arising inwardly in the child. The child will gradually become slow to relate to his own inner activity, and because outer activity is forced on to him, that activity will be hollow for him and he will perform it without interest.

We very much regret that a most unfortunate thing happened with the recording of the lectures. The tape containing the lecture by Dr. Peter Selg, "The Organ of the Heart and the Heart Forces," turned out to be blank and could not be transcribed. Why, nobody knows. Dr. Selg himself could not reconstruct the lecture, but recommends his book about this theme, called *Mysterium Cordis, von der Mysteriumstätte des Menschenherzen* ("Mysterium Cordis, concerning the mystery shrine of the human heart").

—*Brigitte Goldmann, Vienna, April 2006*

Meeting the Other:
The Human Encounter
DR HEINZ ZIMMERMANN

Note: In the lecture, Dr. Zimmermann spoke of the vowel sounds as pro-nounced in German. They are represented in the English translation in italics and should be pronounced as follows: A [ah as in father*], E [ay as in* weigh*], I [ee as in* field*], O [oh as in* open*], and U [oo as in* true*]. The personal pronoun "I" is not italicized.*

Dr. Steiner speaks of pedagogy as an "art of education." Education is an art, and if one would ask what the particular medium of this art is, one could say creating fruitful meetings and making meetings fruitful. How can I create fruitful meetings in the various constellations of parents, colleagues, the board, kindergarten teachers, friends and advisers? What Rudolf Steiner pointed to, in fact, is that meeting the other in a fruitful way is an art. Of course central to all this is creating fruitful meetings with the child.

What is it is that one meets in the child? On the surface one meets all the trappings of our civilization that the child brings along. The child gives us a picture of our civilization, therefore. After that one comes to the par-ticular phenomena of the child's developmental stage, but also a particu-lar set of parents, and the home surroundings. The deepest encounter, however, is with the germinating individual, which has as yet not been able to fully incarnate. Here lies the possibility to meet something which will come to fruition in the future.

Whereas the word *encounter* contains an element of coming up against something, the word *meeting* also means finding common ground, coming together. Both words imply two sides, and in a true meeting there always is back and forth. It is never a one-way street. I always learn as much from the children as the children learn from me. In a true meeting, we always have to be fully present. Real and fruitful meetings always contain elements of the future and the past. There is the future of the child that hasn't arrived yet but is developing, and then there is that which has come into being, that which the child brings along, and especially what the educators bring along: the past. Past and future meet in the present, and that's where the meeting can become fruitful.

If we are trying to see where the past lives in the human being, we must look at the head. When it is only the heads that meet, the result is not likely to be very fruitful. Heads repel one another. You can't embrace with heads, but you can with arms. When you embrace, be it something or somebody, you are clearly dealing with the sphere of the middle, and that's where meeting takes place. Whereas the limbs create the future, the head is the result of the past, and the middle sphere of the heart is where we are really meeting. But no mediation is possible without the two polarities. We cannot quite do without the head. It might seem advantageous, but it just wouldn't work.

An easy way to think of the colors or qualities of different meetings is to think of them in terms of the vowel sounds of A [ah], E [ay], I [ee], O [oh], and U [oo]. There are A meetings, E meetings, I meetings, O meetings, and U meetings, and they are quite different from one another. Imagine somebody comes in with the gesture of A, which doesn't have to be outward, but can be quite inward. Then this person approaches someone else who is in the E gesture. It might not be a pleasant meeting; in fact, it could be quite dramatic. If the other is also A, the result would be an embrace and O would emerge. Or think of the situation where both would be speaking the sound I [ee]. So they express: "I am here — but so am I." And if it then gets combined with the sound E ("Hey, don't mess with me . . .") well, you know how it goes, many different combinations are possible. The nuances and qualities of the sounds are inexhaustible. I would like to take this opportunity to elaborate on the various qualities a bit more.

With the attitude of A I open myself up. I free up the whole sphere of my heart. A means opening up, in wonder and admiration. Next comes the

E. Here we become conscious of something. *A* means being open to the world: this is the gesture of the small child. *E* implies becoming conscious of something, or, when intensified, defending oneself and drawing a line. The sound *I* is an experience of self, down to the earth, standing one's ground, stamping one's feet, and, going up, leading to the knowledge that one is connected to the heavens, to one's higher ego. In the sound *O*, which comes next, everything is turned around. To enter in the sphere of *O* means to connect with the world, to truly commit even. With *O* there is connection, in *U* there is a drawing back and coming back to one's self. Going from sound to sound, there is a development of consciousness, and this path starts with openness. After that we go through wonder, perception, become conscious, find ourselves within ourselves, and go beyond that into the world. After loving embrace, we finally return to ourselves.

Basically this is a path from the periphery to the center and back again, new, into the periphery. It is a breathing process, and, yes, breathing is essential for us as human beings. And therefore one can say that this third quality, the sound *I* also bears within it the character of egotism. But without egotism we wouldn't have the situation of being placed over against something or someone else. Egotism and altruism are like breathing in and out, it is one process. I pour myself out into the world, and then I come back to myself again.

Directly after birth the child still grows up in a peripheral consciousness, that is to say, it first wakes up in the limbs. Those are the first to be awake, and the limbs connect us to the cosmos, where the "I" still lives in the periphery. As the child grows, it gradually awakens in the middle sphere of the heart, and finally the head spirit wakes up, and as soon as the head spirit becomes awake the child becomes unpleasant. Of course it may be unpleasant all the time, but when the head spirit awakens, the unpleasantness stems from that particular stage of development. Now the child will find the hair in the soup, and will notice everything other people do wrong. The head becomes clever and can show you everything you're doing wrong, and is also so smart and dialectically adept that it can argue anything it wants. The head uses thinking to serve the will and will argue past the point where it knows that it is no longer right; but — such arguments can be continued ad infinitum. This is the flip side of the awakening of the power of judgment.

This is the stage where the head wakes up, and at this point, one can say, development could be complete. But that wouldn't be all that pleasant. One has arrived in the head, so to speak, and this is in fact the situation adults are in. From the limbs we have developed through the middle sphere and have now arrived in the head. We couldn't go any further up, it stops with the head. Now is the time to turn around, otherwise one only becomes an egotist. The head is an egotist. If one turns around now, and tries to go the way from the head to the heart, without losing the head, and from there enter into the limbs, one becomes a person who acts out of insight. When that is the case, one makes conscious what the child brings unconsciously. This time, however, the direction is reversed: it has to come out of the future, out of the ideal. And in this way one can meet the child in a fruitful way.

The meeting one can have with a child, especially in the first seven years, is of such a nature. Even though one is awake in the head oneself, one cannot meet the small child through the head. Only when one has built up a new middle sphere from out of the head will one be able to come to a fruitful meeting, whereby one allows oneself to be fructified from out of the future. Thus one can say that the child who is to be educated is an example for the educator. What does the small child, the kindergarten child, have? It has this amazing capacity for wonder, which we as adults no longer have. We have become like a filing system, which can deal with any new experience that meets us; we just file it away. But for the child everything is new. Children have that capacity of admiration, of wonder, of devotion, of learning new things. Just think how many times a child can fall down and get up again! I have never yet heard a child say, "Now I have got enough, I am maxed out." They keep going at something, over and over again, and then they go at it again. It is this tireless repetition, this potential of the will, which we envy as adults. We usually don't have this stamina anymore. So here again the child is an example for us. The will to learn, the capacity for devotion, the ability to admire and be amazed: these are all things which come to us from out of the future through the child.

If we are serious about making our meeting with the child fruitful, we can ask the following question. How do we reach the sources of strength which can fructify us from out of the future, in order to really bring about a meeting such as has been described above? That is to say, when we have consciously transformed ourselves "from the top down."

Here we come to something that I would like to stress especially strongly, namely that there is a type of meeting which fructifies every other meeting. The type of meeting I mean is the meeting with the self, the meeting which often takes place around the first moon node, at the age of eighteen and two thirds. A girl once told me at this age, "I have experienced how the starry skies were completely open, and I know why I have come to earth." That's how she put it. "I know why I have come to the earth. I have a task which is my future and I carry it within me. This is the element which I can experience within myself as a fountain, an inexhaustible source of strength for transformation." One can also have this experience when somebody dies, or when one meets another person or child. These are the moments when one notices that there is more to the "I" than one has in one's head, when one becomes conscious of the "I" which is connected to the periphery, which encircles one, the sphere from which the child gradually grows in the center.

The South American poet Juan Ramon Jimenez captures this moment in a wonderful way:

> I am not I.
> I am this one
> Walking beside me whom I do not see.
> Whom at times I manage to visit,
> And at other times I forget.
> The one who remains silent when I talk,
> The one who forgives, sweet, when I hate,
> The one who takes a walk when I am indoors,
> The one who will remain standing when I die. (Translated by Robert Bly)

This is a wonderful poem about this second, better person in us, the one whom we bring from before birth down to the earth and carry with us after death into the spiritual world. Here lies the source of self-transformation. I can develop faithfulness in this being, faithfulness towards the higher self. It is a fruitful exercise to ask oneself now and again, "Where do I have such gentle experiences, when did I first experience this source, this divine element within me?" This is truly a key to the heavens.

Here we have to deal with opposition from the other "I," which also has meetings. A German colloquial expression for this translates as "I, Incorporated," meaning the ego as an institution, which is so established that it doesn't notice what comes out of the future. Our own soul is the theater for the struggle between these two competing elements. And the fruitfulness of a meeting depends on the state of this struggle.

Maybe you were just on an airplane and happened to be sitting next to a very fat passenger. It often happens. And the question is: how do you react? Only passively? Aloof, maybe, or a little bit territorial? And then there's always the problem of the armrest. Who should use it? There's no space for two people, only one elbow can rest on it. The elbow may even stick out, and how does one handle such a problem? It's the same thing when one stands in line. The Russians are wonderful at this; they can stand in line without getting annoyed. There you can learn to wait, perhaps even start a wonderful conversation, or learn a poem by heart. You can think, "I'm in luck. I am standing in line, at last I have some time." How do I work with a meeting such as the one mentioned above so that I have the feeling, "In this encounter I really come up against the fact that the other person also has a body." And I either look upon the other as a nuisance and would prefer to have him out of the way, or — now comes the opposite — I can rise above this automatic reaction of my physical nature. That will help the meeting be a fruitful one.

Here is a situation teachers are all familiar with. All the children are sitting there with eyes wide open, waiting for the fairy tale. Then comes this boy and throws a black rubber spider on the ground. Of course everybody is yelling and there's quite a drama. What do you do? You can't get annoyed. You have to keep your composure! Easier said than done. And then you get annoyed about the annoyance you feel rising up within you because it's always the same child, you have discussed it with his parents and they don't see any problem.

This is a case of coming up against spontaneous sympathy or antipathy. One can be justly annoyed, and it may be that the only way to meet is through a confrontation. Of course it isn't possible in such spontaneous situations to simply let it go by and see what happens. But the question is whether one leaves it at antipathy, because that way one doesn't get any further with the child. That's when the head would get in the way again. The question becomes: how do I deal with my inborn antipathies and sympathies? Do I let them be what they are, or do I transform them?

In every community there will be somebody who especially annoys you — you only have to hear the person's voice and you're annoyed. For example you already know from the moment the person opens her mouth: "I will definitely contradict this. That is for sure, whatever it is she actually says, she just gets on my nerves. And then this hat, and this dumb pullover, and always these colors — just awful!" Well, you all know how it goes. People appear in your life, and when they do, you avoid them. How do we deal with these things? How would it be if we would start to play from the moment we had our first negative encounter? Play is the most holy and beautiful thing a child sets an example with.

In this year we celebrate the 200th anniversary of the death of an important champion of the spirit, Friedrich Schiller. It was he who wrote down the most beautiful thoughts about playing that have ever been formulated. Taking the child as an example, he applies his observations to adults. In the so-called "Letters concerning the Aesthetic Education of the Human Being" he writes, "The human being plays only when he is human in the fullest sense of the word and he is only fully human when playing." So the most human activity is play.

What does Schiller mean by play? He also applies the concept of play to the art of meeting, which he calls an art of living, of which the art of education is a subdivision. This in fact is a component of a future social art. Schiller concludes that we are always engaged in a struggle between two drives which are constantly at war with one another and suppress one another. The first drive comes from the senses, which causes our desires, joy in life, our cravings — for chocolate and all manner of delicious things — and the second drive comes from the side of reason and creates form. It is the latter that tells us, "You may not have that, when you eat too much chocolate you will get fat." That is the other drive, originating more in the spiritual side of our natures, the drive to shape and form, whereas the force of desire stems from the senses.

Schiller describes a concrete situation in which this war between the two drives is taking place: "When we find our our passions embracing someone who deserves our loathing, we painfully experience nature's coercive power."

Imagine falling in love with someone you know is a scoundrel. But you're in love; what can you do? That's when you feel the coercive power of nature, when you know you shouldn't, but the desire is there.

Another situation: "When we feel inimical towards another person," so when we feel antipathy towards someone else, "who commands our respect, we experience the coercive power of the reason as painful." So imagine being in a college of teachers, or in a kindergarten meeting, and here is one of your colleagues, and it happens to be the one you could do without, and she has just scored a big success. What do you do now? Of course you have the option to smile wryly and say, "That was very beautiful . . ." Reason forces me to say, "I have to acknowledge that." Of course I have to, but I am gnashing my teeth all the same.

That is the starting point. In both cases I am not free. In the one case I have to obey reason, which forces me to get over my antipathy, which I don't really want to conquer. In the other case it is nature which forces me to love somebody who doesn't deserve it, who isn't worth it. How do I get out of this dilemma?

The way out is through play. This is the point where I should begin to play. Of course this takes time. Learning to play an instrument takes quite a bit of practice, as we know from learning to play the violin. We must practice until we become free from our antipathies, so that we can say, "Here comes antipathy again, but no, I don't want it right now!" It takes a lot of practice to get that far. But this practice bears fruit and is even enjoyable. The more one has one's own emotions in hand, so that they don't overpower one, one will feel more and more a sense of sovereignty. Likewise one shouldn't be terrorized by reason, but decide anew in each situation. That is when one begins to play in Schiller's sense. Playing in this sense means dealing imaginatively with either respect for others or natural inclinations, in such a way that I can feel in charge and act freely, which will bring me to a new level. I would now like to sum this up briefly.

By way of conclusion, here is a schematic representation of what we have been talking about.

$$
\begin{array}{ccc}
& I & \\
\textit{Sympathy} & - & \textit{Antipathy} \\
\textit{Limbs} & - & \textit{Head} \\
\textit{Altruism} & - & \textit{Egotism} \\
\textit{Will} & - & \textit{Mental Picture} \\
& I &
\end{array}
$$

We breathe between these two polarities all the time, and this is symbolized in the lemniscate. It is not true that sympathy is good and antipathy is bad. Neither is egotism bad or altruism good. Altruism can even take on a highly negative form. You are probably familiar with people — in anthroposophical circles also — who are sacrificing themselves twenty-four hours a day. Smoke from the incense is rising all the time. "I do all this for the cause and I'm going under; I am dying for all this." This is obviously intolerable, it is unhealthy. After all, one has to come back to one's self, one cannot remain in the O gesture all the time, there comes a time one has to return to one's self, to the I vowel-gesture and create a balance between E and O. I — assertion, O — giving out. So these saints who sacrifice themselves — we don't want those, they lead to burnout. We are striving for a balance. However, balance has to be accompanied by something else, and this brings us to yet another step. I will now read the rest of the Schiller quotation: "As soon as we turn our inclination to the other with interest, and as soon as we have come to respect him, the coercion both of the senses and of reason disappears."

What does that mean? I begin to become interested in the one who is so unsympathetic to me, and when I'm interested, I begin to come out of myself and enter into the other. Interest means "to be in between." I will no longer be with my self, but with the other.

And then I might begin to ask: "Where does he come from? What is the destiny of this other person?" I begin to become interested, and will begin to feel a certain acquired inclination towards the person I didn't want to see. This is no longer spontaneous sympathy, but an inclination acquired by active interest. This is the one side, and the other side is respect. Even in the depths of depravity I can discover something precious. I learn to discover what is hidden behind the obvious. To win through to respect means to learn to value the capacities of the other, and in learning to value those, I will also create a new relationship. This is only possible, however, when one frees oneself from spontaneous antipathy. Antipathy tends to be tied to the past and bound to the body; when I loosen those ties I can come to free play within the pattern of meeting the other. This play originates in the "I" of the adult. And now comes the last stage: "And we begin to love the other." Love in this sense is the crown. Thus we can come to see free play as a way of liberating ourselves from the inherent disposition of our souls, from the temperament, and so forth. The result will be love. Love is not an enhanced form of altruism, it is a highly advanced playing together, the highest form of the interplay between egotism and altruism. One could say, love has gone through *A*, *E*, and *U*, and only then comes to *O*. That is to say, once one has experienced who one is, one can come to love. Therefore we can come to see love not as the starting point, but as the aim of a development of free play. Here we have the free human being, and now we can write in our summary: The "I," which is playing in the middle, in the heart.

Here we have the corresponding form of children's play for adults. When I observed one of my godchildren playing with bottles and cans, which he did over a period of time, I noticed that he always formed a beautiful half circle. At one point this stopped, and lo and behold, the teeth came. And then came a time in which he played with hundreds of cards, in such a way that he always turned each card two times around before putting it down: the brain convolutions. This mysterious process of building up the bodily sheath from out of the periphery is reflected in play. It was wonderful to observe this correspondence, which of course underwent a metamorphosis later on, around the age of three or four; it started even earlier. The educator has to conclude from this that the child has to be given the opportunity to express what wells up from within, unconsciously. The adult, by contrast, must do this consciously, out of free will. The result will be play as Schiller meant it. And when "we begin to love the other," we meet the child again, but on a higher level. That is what meeting from out of the future means, meeting from a place where ideas have been made into ideals. And that can only happen when one uses the head in such a way that it directs the heart and limbs rightly.

One can develop the above-mentioned capacities by doing practical exercises. I would like to describe two of those briefly here. Rudolf Steiner calls such exercises *Praktische Menschenkunde*, which may be translated as "practical knowledge of the human being," or "applied Anthroposophy." Try in the evening to think back on the handshake of people you have met that day. How did you experience the hands? Or perhaps only the hand of one person, maybe of one child at the beginning of the period and at the end. Or the eyes, or the way the person walks. These things are difficult to observe. This is about developing interest in people, by focusing on one aspect and forming a relationship to the child that way, a connection which doesn't originate in a naturally felt affinity, but one which originates in a question arising out of a desire to know more about the human being.

Then there is listening as a further way to practice, so that one gradually comes away from oneself more and more, but is more out there with the other person. In his book *How to Know Higher Worlds* Rudolf Steiner writes the following words:

> *When one practices listening without criticism, even in cases where an opinion is brought forward which is entirely contrary to one's own, one will gradually learn to become one with the being of another person, and to fully enter into that person's world. One will learn to penetrate below the surface and hear the soul of the other behind the words.*

"Behind the words . . ." every human being has a unique voice, and by entering into that voice a communion takes place; a connection is formed with the being of the other. In another context, Rudolf Steiner calls this the "mystery of compassion."

The best place to start practicing is to choose the person who annoys you most, or to pick a person you normally don't pay much attention to. By doing this, we build up a connection which will become fruitful in the future. We have some encounters that are brought about by the past; our legs simply carry us to the people concerned. But there are also encounters that I can consciously cultivate and make fruitful that way. In exactly the same way I can learn from encounters and in doing so make future encounters fruitful as well. Digesting the experience will make future meetings more fruitful.

I would like to conclude my contribution by telling you two little stories. The first story — both have been changed a little bit — stems from India.

After God had created the whole world, including human beings, he sent the human beings down to earth. But they didn't enjoy the earth all that much and soon came back again. They returned to heaven much too early, and God really didn't want to have them come back that soon. So he thought to himself, "What can I do now?" and after pondering this he came up with the following idea. He thought, "I simply have to close the heavens. Only the question is, "Where should I hide the key?" For people are smart, and they will look everywhere. Even if I would sink it to the bottom of a vast ocean, they would find it." And finally he had the splendid idea to put the key in the heart of the human being. Within every human being there lies the key to the heavens, and it can be found when one seeks the way to the heart. This is what self-transformation from out of the future means: it has to come from the heavenly being within each human being.

The second story is the story of a dying monastery (or perhaps to make it more current, we could say an anthroposophical "branch"). The members are all over seventy, and only five of them are left in this monastic community. A friend arrives, and together with the Abbot he laments the situation. "We are doing what we have always been doing, but no new people are coming." We know how this is, it is a familiar dirge, which might sound somewhat like this: "We are doing the same thing, only the students have become so different." So the two of them are complaining together about the terrible decadence of present-day civilization, and how the end is in sight.

On leaving, the friend says, "I can only wish you luck, but one thing I would still like to say to you. There is one among you, who is blessed by God." (In the anthroposophical branch one would perhaps say "an initiate," or that this person "had special spiritual gifts.") With that, the friend takes his leave and the five are alone again.

Now all of them are beginning to think. "Now who could that can be? The Abbot? Could it be I? Who knows, it isn't out of the question. But I don't really think so, maybe it is Brother Felix? Or someone else?" And while they are all thinking about this, their thoughts create a special form of respect, because anyone could be the chosen one after all. Because of this, they build up a cohesion which radiates from the community to such an extent that new people are attracted. The result is that the monastery blossoms again and acquires new members.

So this second story is also wonderful. What it implies is that we can discover that a divine source dwells within every other human being, and when we actively cultivate this fact within ourselves, we will also be able to work together in a different way instead of only seeing one another as acting in "typical" ways, this way or that way. Instead, we can say, "No, it is not 'typical'; within this person's 'type,' something unassailably divine expresses itself, something from out of the future, a seed, which is the child within every human being, just like the child who comes into the kindergarten to us in the morning."

This discovery is wonderfully expressed by the philosopher Martin Buber. He says, "On the way to becoming I, I say: You." On the way to becoming myself, in the process of becoming "I," I see the other.

Returning to our starting point, the art of education as a social art, we can say that, within the circle of the Seven Arts, education is architecture turned inside out. We can think of this metamorphosis in the following way. By building a temple or a church we create a place where the divine can dwell; we create a house for a specific God. The social art of education is a process which takes place in time. It is not a spatial process like architecture, and that's where the reversal lies. We try to discover the divine in the other, because we have discovered it in ourselves and reckon with it daily, because this is the source of everything, of the way we treat the children and any human being for that matter. Our effort with the children is to allow their different sheaths to develop in such a way that each one's unique individuality will be able to come to the fore in the best possible way. Respecting one's own higher source forms the prerequisite for discovering the higher self of the other, and to believe in it, to remain faithful to it, even when there are lapses — that is what education and life are about.

The Healing Power of Play

JOAN ALMON

As a Waldorf kindergarten teacher I had the opportunity to travel around the world for Waldorf education and to meet many teachers, parents, and children in different countries. I was in Tanzania, in Africa, a few years ago, and there was a Waldorf school with two kindergartens. One of the teachers had already been in a Waldorf teacher training in East Africa, and her kindergarten was going very nicely. The children were playing quite well.

The other teacher was quite new to Waldorf education. She had only started a month before and was not yet in a training course. She was very gifted in playing with children, one on one, or with a small group of children, but she truly did not know what to do with twenty-five children. And you know how chaotic a kindergarten can be if the children are not playing well. When I went past her room that first day I could hear the sounds of chaos. I knew them well from my own early years as a teacher. On the second day, I was going to have a couple of hours to be with her in the kindergarten, and I thought: "What can I do in two hours that could help her?"

The next morning, when I entered her room the children were outside playing, and I said to her: "Usually I bring sewing with me when I visit a kindergarten so that I have work to do in front of the children, but on this trip I did not bring my sewing kit. Do you have some work that I could do, such as making a doll, or repairing a play cloth?" She looked very puzzled and said: "Oh no, I do all of that work at home in the evening." I was shocked and replied, "No, no, in a Waldorf kindergarten we do that work in front of the children to inspire their play." I looked around her room for something that I could do when the children came in. There weren't many supplies in the kindergarten, but the children were making little pom-poms with yarn and cardboard, and she had a little basket of leftover yarn pieces. They were quite small, perhaps only a half meter in length.

When the children came in, I was sitting at a table winding tiny little balls from the yarn, singing a song about winding the yarn. As each ball was finished, I set it down forming a little circle of balls. This is a little trick that I learned from Freya Jaffke years ago. When you want to engage children in play, you can slowly create a little circle of stones or wood pieces for them. Quite often, by the time the circle is finished, the child has an idea for play and is ready to continue on his or her own. I did that often in my kindergarten when a child did not have an idea of what to play, and it nearly always helped.

So I made these little yarn balls, and all the children gathered around to watch. What happened next was amazing to me. When the circle was finished the children turned like a flock of birds and went into every part of the room and began to play. They took chairs and made a bus, they built shops with play stands, and they made houses.

There was one boy that the teacher had pointed out to me the day before, saying, "He cannot play at all; he only hits children and disturbs their play, or he stays by himself." He now built himself a little play area with a table and some little pieces of wood on top. He also put a small cabinet behind him. I don't usually ask children what they are playing, but in this case, I wanted to understand him a little more and only had this one chance.

After a while I went over to him and asked: "What are you playing?" He answered, "This is an airplane and I'm the pilot." I helped to build up his play space with some playstands and cloth to give him a greater sense of protection and asked him what was in the cabinet behind him. "The television," he answered. I had suspected that television viewing was part of his problem, and now I was fairly sure. The teachers were so happy to see him playing at last.

What was especially beautiful, though, was that the next day when I stopped by to say goodbye on my way to the airport, the children were again deep in play. There was that wonderful hum in the kindergarten that comes when children are deep in play. The little boy who had played pilot and who had been so unsocial was now taking the pom-poms that still had holes in the middle. He put yarn through the holes and made necklaces for the children in the class. He had found a way to connect with them. He went from one child to the next, giving each of them a necklace to wear. The power of children's imitation and the real work of the teacher are a powerful combination which lead children deep into the world of play. They can also bring children back to play if they have forgotten how to play.

Imitation in early childhood is an incredible gift. It is a gift that the children bring down to earth with them. When we human beings are in the spiritual world, we breathe our way out into the hierarchies, we take them into ourselves. This is how we learn from higher beings.

This capacity to flow out into the hierarchies is a capacity we bring down to earth with us. In the heavenly world we interpenetrate with higher beings. When we bring this to earth we call it imitation. The child has the ability to breathe into us and "take us on." Imitation is the basis of the religious life of the child, a religious life which includes the spiritual world, but is very focused on the earthly world. Imitation is the child's way of communing with others.

There are indications from Rudolf Steiner that we kindergarten teachers are like priests in the kindergarten. One can easily misunderstand that indication. Normally, the priest is at the altar, looking up, as it were, to the spiritual world. We are at the worktable bringing spiritual impulses down into the earthly world. This is the world into which children are incarnating, and we are there to help them. They bring wonderful gifts with them. One is the ability to meet us in the world of imitation, to enter deeply into us, to try us on as if we were a kind of clothing for them to enter into us as we bake, or sew, or do woodworking. As we work they enter into us, not just our outer gestures, as important as they are, but they enter into our whole inner mood and being.

Maybe you have experienced in your kindergarten what I experienced, that on some days there was a kind of nervous energy in the room. The children were playing, but their play didn't have that deep hum of the kindergarten. I would look around from my work area, to see if someone was creating a disturbance, but no, they were all playing. Nobody was really disturbed, and yet there was a nervousness in the air. Finally I learned an important lesson: that when I experienced that nervousness I needed to first look at myself, at my own inner mood. Often I found that I had grown nervous and was not calm and focused. I was listening to the class while I worked, but I was not fully focused on them or on my work. I was thinking of other things. When I became attentive again, the whole class became quieter and more focused in their play.

Young children are so open to our every mood, and we live together with them in an intimate way through their capacity for imitation. They take us in, they breathe into us, and we can help them to grow and flourish. We can help them to become full human beings.

There is something else that lives strongly in the child and is a gift of the hierarchies, a gift for the child's incarnation. It is a deep wisdom that lives in each child and shows them what they need for their path of incarnation. One sees it already in the infant. How does that little baby, lying there on its stomach, know that it needs to lift its head and look around? Yet every healthy baby does that at a certain point. How does a baby know, when it is on its back and rather helpless, that it needs to fling its arm over and turn itself over? No one is teaching this to the baby. It's not even imitation in the direct sense, because it is not seeing people do this.

Yet a baby of six months old has a deep inner wisdom that is time to turn over. I often think of Gordon, a little six-month-old baby whose family lived with us for a month. I used to come home from kindergarten every day and relax by watching Gordon on the rug on his back trying to turn over. It took him the whole month to learn to turn over. Every day, over and over, he'd fling his arm over trying to turn himself. He'd do it dozens of time, perhaps hundreds of times, but never with a hint of frustration. Finally, one day, he did it. To us it felt like an enormous deed. But for him it was normal. He practiced it a few times more as if to be sure he could do it, and then he seemed ready to take on the next step of development. In this sense there is no pause in your development when you are little. You just keep going from one step to the next. All the while there is a tremendous inner wisdom that guides you from one step to the next.

When we see children at play, we also see this wisdom at work before our eyes. We see it in the normal development of play, but it is clearest when a child has a problem in life and uses play to resolve that problem. I want to give you a few examples, and I am sure you will know many, many more from your own experiences.

There was a little boy who came into my kindergarten who was about four years old, and the first thing I noticed was that he had an unusual voice. His speech was well developed, but his voice was that of a baby or a very young child. It didn't fit his age of development. I had not experienced this situation before, and I wasn't sure what it was that I was seeing in him. I watched his play, and every day he played in the same way. He took six or seven stumps and he'd make himself a small round house with the stumps standing up. Then he'd go into the house, and he'd put a cloth cover over the top of the house. The house had no doors and no windows. Every day he built the same house and spent almost all of his playtime in it.

I had a conference with his mother to try to understand what was happening in his life. She also was very concerned about him. He had been fine up until age three and a half. Then a baby sister was born, and at first he was fine about that as well. But when the baby was about six months old and was in a very cute stage, it seemed that everybody was drawn to the baby and not so drawn to the older child. At that point he began to regress, to go backwards and to develop a form of baby language. He also wanted to drink from a bottle again. One day when I looked inside his house, I saw that he was curled up like a baby in a womb, and I thought: "He has made himself a womb; he has gone as far back as he can, as if he was still inside his mother."

It concerned me but my sense was that he knew what he was doing, and that something was in a growth process in him and not stuck. I felt I needed to give him time to work through this. It took about two or three months in which he played the same way every day. My assistant and I watched over him and did not let the other children disturb his play.

After a few months a day came when he left a little opening in his house. It was not very big, but it was important. Then, a couple of days later, he made a bigger opening, and then he went out looking for a friend. He found a lovely boy named Bill and brought him into his house with him. There they played for a few days. Then the house seemed too cramped, and it began to grow. It grew bigger and bigger, and other children could come in. Slowly the child's voice came back to normal. Young children have a wisdom about what they need. They cannot verbalize it to us, but they often show us their wisdom through play.

Here is one other example. There was a four-year-old girl who came into my kindergarten. She was very sweet and very playful. The only thing that concerned me about her was her voice, but the problem was in the opposite direction of the little boy I described. Hers was not a baby voice, but a high-pitched, nervous voice. I have to admit that her voice got on my nerves. It was hard for me to open my heart fully when she would approach me. Something in me would draw back as she approached me, and I had to work to overcome that.

One day she brought me one of our little knot dolls, just a simple little cloth doll. With it she brought a thin play cloth, a very long cloth, at least four meters long. She asked me to wrap her baby, and my first reaction was: "She should go and get me a smaller cloth." My second reaction was: "Let's wait and see." And so I took the doll and I took the cloth and I began to wrap the doll, very slowly. I thought: "Soon she will be impatient, and then I will go faster." Slowly, slowly, I swaddled the baby. She was not impatient. She seemed to take in every gesture, every wrapping of the baby. She waited till the last bit of cloth was used and then took her baby doll back again. After that, her voice came down into a normal range. It was as if she herself needed to be wrapped, as if she was too exposed to the world, and it was making her nervous. Through this simple wrapping of the doll and all that went into it, I think she now felt wrapped and protected.

I want to tell you one more story, and it goes in a slightly different direction. In this case I felt the children were showing something of their development, but it was going in an unhealthy direction, and I had to decide what to do about it.

Two little boys, Brendan and Thomas, were good friends and played together every day for several years. Now they were five years old. Brendan, a radiant, large-headed child, was very playful. He was an exceptionally imaginative and social child. Thomas was a little more drawn into himself and was a little more stressed by life. But he was also a very sweet child. They played happily together and with other children. When they were about five and a half, you could see their intellects beginning to wake up. Children at that age often, out of themselves, become very interested in arithmetic, in mathematics. In my experience, the girls often become interested in infinity, and will have huge philosophical conversations about infinity, while the boys become interested in mathematical problems. Brendan and Thomas woke up to arithmetic at the same time, and often, over the snack table, they would throw arithmetic problems at each other. It was playful, and I let it be.

In their play, however, they entered a phase of very intense activity with each other. They went to an area where there were playstands forming a house-like structure, and they took over that area. Usually the playstands were moved and rearranged into new houses, shops, puppet theaters and much more. But they took over this area and did not move the play stands. Instead, they took a basket of ropes and tied ropes on the top of the play stands. They used many ropes, and tied many, many knots. You know how children can get into tying knots at that age. I don't know at what age they learn to untie knots, but it is not in the kindergarten. Clean-up became difficult with so many knots to be untied, and I will confess that I finally put a pair of scissors in my pocket to quietly cut through the knots.

Every day they played this way, and they would not let anybody else into their play. It was a picture for me of the awakening intellect in the boys, like a spider spinning a web of thoughts. Gradually I felt this intellectual development and all these knotty thoughts were holding them in and pressing them down rather than allowing them to grow and flourish. They were awakening to thinking, but their thoughts were not taking them out into world. These thoughts were not leading them toward an interest in others. This was a form of intellectual development that was isolating them, as if they had climbed an "ivory tower" and cut themselves off from others. I began to grow very uncomfortable about their play.

One morning, before they came, I took the basket of ropes and I put it high up on a shelf out of their reach. I expected the boys to be very upset, even angry. They came and asked me for the ropes, and I said to them: "Today, the ropes are going to rest." What I felt in them was not anger but a huge relief. They were not at all upset. They actually seemed grateful, as if they were relieved of a burden they could not overcome by themselves. That day they went and played by themselves in the house, but the next day a few children came into the house and played with them. After a few days, they were again in a normal flow of play with the children.

Then they came to me and asked for the ropes. What was I going to do? I trusted that they were now in a new place, and I brought the ropes down and gave them to them. Now a whole new play developed. They took the ropes and used them as telephone wires, and they connected all the play houses in the kindergarten. They linked all the children together into one large social network. All that thinking and intellect that had felt trapped inside was now working itself out into a large social body. The other children helped, as well, to create this phone system that united all their houses.

For me, this was a real lesson that even when one fully appreciates the wisdom of children's play, one still has to practice a kind of discernment, a subtle form of judgment. Not all play is equally healthy for children. When is the play supporting the child's blossoming and growing, and when is it taking hold almost like an addiction, a habit that's not healthy?

It is not always easy to discern what is healthy and what is not in children's play, but as Waldorf teachers we can cultivate discernment through our inner work, our schooling path as adults. I think of many wonderful exercises that Rudolf Steiner has given us that help develop our inner capacity for discernment, for telling the difference between one thing and another. I would like to describe just one of those exercises. It is one where he says: "Observe the plant world, that which is blossoming and growing, and that which is fading and decaying."

You can practice this outdoors or even indoors when you watch a bouquet of flowers in your own room. Perhaps there are flower buds in the bouquet, and other flowers that are just starting to open, while others are in full bloom, and still others are fading and decaying. You can sense the tremendous capacity to grow in the bud and the strength of growth in the opening flower. But as the flower passes its peak, its petals thin and begin to droop. They are no longer so life-filled and gradually they drop off. Over and over you do these exercises and gradually you sense in a child: "This child is in a budding, opening process, or this child is drooping and not thriving. Or perhaps this child is fading, but it feels appropriate, as if it is shedding an old skin and making way for a new one."

I would like to tell you one more story about Brendan, the little boy with the ropes. He went off to a public school, and I lost track of him until about five years ago. Then there was a big article about Brendan in the newspaper. He was about seventeen years old, in the twelfth grade of a public high school. From the article you could see that he was a wonderful, warm young fellow. But he had a severe health problem, and this problem was that he had used computers so much that he had intense pain in his wrists and arms. The pain was so severe that he could no longer hold a pencil or pen to write. Someone had to sit next to him to take notes for him in class. He was not allowed to use a computer, and even opening a door was extremely painful for him.

The journalist, knowing that Brendan was going to go to Harvard University the next year, called the health service at Harvard to ask: "Do you have other students with this problem?" The University said: "Yes. We've didn't have this problem in the past, but right now we have about a hundred students on campus with this problem. They developed the problem from using computers too much." In Brendan's case I wished so much that someone would have seen that he was trapped in his relationship with a computer and helped him out before he did himself such harm. For me it was as if he had spun a web again and gotten stuck in it. Finally the world of computers had to be closed, at least for a while, to let him breathe into the world again. It's hard sometimes to see these things and to say no to a child: "No, not now, this is not the right thing, this is too much." But that is part of what we learn as teachers, and we need to help parents learn it as well.

Play is a force that allows children to grow in every area of their being. It is a foundation for all their learning, and it allows them to explore every aspect of life, including those that hold real sorrows and problems for them. Therefore it's a huge tragedy that we hear from all sides that play, creative, open play, is disappearing from children's lives. This is a theme that I am very actively working on in the United States through the Alliance for Childhood. In this first stage of our work we are gathering stories from teachers, and I will tell you just one.

A professor of early childhood education in Boston told me of a workshop she did at a NAEYC conference. It was a year after 9/11 and she was asking the teachers if they saw an increase in violent play in their kindergartens. There was an uncomfortable buzzing in the room as they began to speak with each other. She asked what was wrong, and one teacher spoke up and said: "The problem is not that we see more violent play, the problem is that we no longer see children playing at all." She asked if others had a similar experience and about ninety percent of the two hundred teachers put up their hands.

The Alliance then did a small study where graduate students asked experienced kindergarten teachers about play. Two things became clear. One, the curriculum of our kindergartens in the U.S. no longer allows any time for free play. Most of our kindergartens are now full-day kindergartens, from nine o'clock to three o'clock. Reading and writing, mathematics and science, fill the children's day, and these five-year-olds have no time for play. The other thing that became clear was that when the teachers gave children time to play, the children did not know what to do. "They have no ideas of their own," said the teachers.

We then went in search of more research. Was there any quantitative research about the disappearance of play? That was our question. We found one excellent researcher who had studied the lives of children by asking teachers and parents to keep a diary for a day, writing down every thirty minutes what the children were doing. Thousands of these diaries were collected, and all of the answers were very clearly coded so you could see how much time was spent eating, how much time was spent sleeping, and how much time was spent playing. We asked her if she had found a decline in children's play and were astonished when she said, no, she had found an increase. "How is that possible?" we asked. "Everyone is telling us that there is a loss of play."

Then I had a thought and asked, "What do you include under play?" She answered, "Outdoor play, make-believe-play and computer play." Aha. Computer play had increased considerably over the five-year time period, so we asked her if each of the forms of play had been coded separately? She said they were and we asked if she would separate the different types of play and look specifically for changes in the time spent in make-believe play. We found that time spent in indoor creative play had indeed decreased significantly in the five years of the study. Her data will be available in fall 2007.

Though we may not always know the figures, from all sides we hear reports that there is less and less imaginative play taking place in children's lives. The Alliance has received funding for research to help fill in the picture. Meanwhile, we are addressing the real challenge: "How do we bring play back?" We're working with a very skilled "playworker" from London's Adventure Playgrounds, and with her help we've been carrying the message of play into children's museums, parks, preschools and kindergartens, and many other venues. I'm happy to say there is growing interest in play although there is a long way to go before it is restored to all children's lives.

While play is still alive in many countries, we hear reports of its fading away. So often what we we experience in the United States is like an epidemic that goes around the world. The disappearance of play will also will go around the world unless we find ways to change the situation. We need to become fully active in support of the spirit of play.

I often ask myself: "What can we do?" I think of the things that we can do — and I mean "we," because all of you as Waldorf early childhood educators are experts in play. Sometimes you don't realize how much you know about play, but you have real expertise in this area and can use that expertise to help rescue play. What could that mean? In the first instance it can mean workshops for parents on play so they become strong in their support of play for their children. My favorite workshop that I did for parents was where I brought them into the kindergarten and let them play. It's a unique experience for them and one they valued.

In this workshop the parents did not only talk about play, they actually played in the simplest ways. They built houses, dressed up, played with dolls, and much more. At first they were self-conscious, but gradually they relaxed and really played. Afterwards they said they were astonished to realize that this type of play was still alive in them, for they thought it had died out long ago.

Also, I've helped to organize Play Days, and can recommend these. This is where you create a play situation, indoors or out, on a Saturday morning, let's say, and you invite in the public so that children and adults can come and play. You don't do this for the sake of bringing in more families to your school, although that might result, but really to support play itself, to help people understand the importance and the joy of play. Play is a joyful human experience, and we've lost the sense for that. Play Days show parents the importance and fun of play. For information on planning Play Days, see the Web site of the International Play Association: www.ipausa.org.

There are many other things that can be done to support play and help bring it back. If you like to write, then write an article for your newspaper or a local magazine about play. What if all over the world, in the 1400 Waldorf kindergartens, one deed was done each year just for the purpose of supporting play? And what if we brought along friends from other kindergartens, non-Waldorf kindergartens, and encouraged them to do the same? I think we could stop this decline of play. We could reverse this tendency. I know we are all so busy with what we are already doing, but my biggest concern at the moment is that if we do not find ways to become active in support of play, then its disappearance will spread and grow, and year by year children will play less and less until they have forgotten how to play altogether. And with that loss will go one of the most powerful elements in children's development and one of the most important forms of healing that children have available for themselves. This loss of healing will happen at the very time when new illnesses, psychological illnesses, are growing intensively in children. Already the World Health Organization has issued a kind of call saying that by 2020 there will be an enormous increase in mental illness in children around the world. Mental illness is growing rapidly among children, and play is a strong "medicine" for children. It can lower their stress levels and help them deal with their problems, yet it is disappearing just when children need it so badly.

Children need play for a dozen reasons, for a hundred reasons. It is their doorway to growth and learning, and it is their doorway to healing. Now we need to make sure that it remains a strong part of their lives.

Acceleration, Retardation, and Healthy Development

DR MICHAELA GLÖCKLER

During the last twenty-five years a lot of research has been done which comes under the general heading of support, be it support for the less gifted and for children with challenges, or support for cases of "dissociative development," in cases where there has been a combination of retardation on the one hand and acceleration on the other. A great deal of research has been done to make clear how to educate children in situations where they have been heavily traumatized.

The textbook I used as a student, three fat volumes on pediatrics, only contained a single sentence about healthy development, and, in fact, not much more is known at the present moment. That sentence runs like this:

Development: a positive definition of optimal life conditions meets with considerable difficulties . . . because the case histories of people who achieve remarkable things later on in life show no similarities which are worth mentioning; at least there is no marked absence of pathogenic influences.

Simply put, we have no scientific data concerning this. That is to say, until recently, for in recent years there has been a change. People are searching for a science that can tell us something about health, about optimal conditions in life, about so-called salutogenesis. But we are not there yet. When one asks the question, "What would optimal life conditions look like?" one will come to the startling realization that it is possible to in fact make children unhappy, stress them and torment them, and witness how they develop well in spite of that! "You had a happy childhood? Too bad! Then there was nothing by which you had to prove yourself!" That is how one book researching the topic of resilience puts it.

There is an incredible amount of material which points in this direction. A strong individuality finds his or her way, and highly remarkable people, when asked about their childhood, will say "Don't touch it!" And yet this is no reason to say, "Therefore we have to torment our children in order for them to come to something!" But it is important to be clear about one thing: development is a mystery, and there are always three components which we can distinguish. The well-known book *Separate Lives: Why Siblings are so Different* by Judy Dunn was the first to elaborate on this in the 1980s. Not only do heredity, neurology, and genes play their role, nor is the environment, the circumstances under which the child grows up, the main determinant. There is that crucial third factor. It emerges when we look at what happens in relationships between individuals. The outcome can be unique and make all the difference.

A young man's background may be a set of the most difficult of circumstances. And then he meets that one person who believes in him, trusts him, and he finds his way. The opposite can also be the case: the most favorable circumstances, the most beautiful Waldorf kindergarten but an individuality who, from within, by destiny, puts obstacle upon obstacle in his own way. And for that reason we must rely in education on some basic preliminaries, things which come first in Waldorf pedagogy. To begin with, every educator should form an inner picture of what health is, of the healthy human being. Secondly, as educators we must accept children the way they come to us. We must recognize them for what they are, and be willing to accompany them on their special path. Thirdly, it will be good to have as clear an idea as possible of one's own development, of one's aims in life and of one's own self-education. When these things are in place, the best results can be expected.

To illustrate this I will give an example that might also serve as a stimulus to work even more in this vein in the kindergarten in the future. I am indebted to a kindergarten teacher for a whole dossier of wonderful descriptions of children in her care. They are case histories in which she describes the way her children developed in her kindergarten. Here is an example:

> *Marcus was already seven when he came to us. According to the mother, he had attended a kindergarten that had labeled him as behaviorally*

disturbed. They had regarded him as a candidate for special education, and he had been treated accordingly. He had often been told in so many words, and his own words confirmed this: "I am stupid anyway; I will end up in the special needs school for sure; nobody likes me anyway."

The mother tells me that the stressful circumstances in the family never let up, what with four unruly boys, a father who drinks, and a mother who is very soft and cannot set boundaries. In their neighborhood they are branded as socially dysfunctional.

I cannot give the full documentation here. Suffice it to say that when Marcus enters the kindergarten at age seven, he behaves like a three-year-old. The kindergarten teacher describes how he catches up slowly but surely. His movement and coordination, speech development and drawing all improve. In the end he actually makes a jump in his development, and she succeeds because she believes in the boy and always carries him in her consciousness.

She describes the situation both from the outside, the changes that occur in the child, and from the inside, her inner workings with the child. He was also very aggressive and it was always a struggle with him to find opportunities where he could succeed in being good and to bring this to his attention, these periods in which his good will shone.

At the end of the report it says:

During the last quarter of the year, Marcus's behavior was truly exemplary for most of the time. It was moving to witness how he turned around. He was able to carry out what he intended to do. It seemed that he took the strength to achieve this from his relationship with me. In the end he managed to also maintain good behavior without my being present. It is a pity that he is almost eight already. If he could have remained here for another year, it would have given us the opportunity to anchor his good behavior more and to stabilize this trend, because it is a great help for him to have people who are guarding him the way we do here.

But now Marcus was taken into the Waldorf school. First he reverted to his old behavior, because the transition was a little too early, which his kindergarten teacher had sensed. But he had a teacher who had taken him into her class in spite of, or actually because of his very difficulties, and he was able to go back to his previous good behavior, and to keep himself in check. Intellectually he came up to grade level in the third year of school, after which he transferred to a public school, and in 2003 he completed his training in a vocational school. At present he intends to become a nurse and is confident about his future.

If one reads any modern book on pediatrics to find out what the current thinking is around the question "What supports development?" one finds a general awareness of important factors. I will list a few. Good care of pregnant women and newborns is generally recognized to be of prime importance. Then comes the importance of support for parents in the education of their children. Parents need instruction in how to find their role as parents in an education that takes the individuality of the child into account. They need help in recognizing the way individuality comes out in certain behaviors and in accepting the manifestation of the individuality of the children in their care.

Dear friends, this doesn't mean that one has to do something special for each individual child; on the contrary! Life may seem a straightforward affair in one sense, but the way children relate to life is endlessly varied. On the one hand the teacher deals with a group of children, but in her heart the teacher has to be conscious of how each individual child is developing. And because one sees the children as individuals, the children will feel recognized individually, even when one does the same thing for all of them. Then one can also have different reactions to different children, according to the way each child behaves. Experience teaches us that children will provoke and remain highly offensive until they feel understood by us. It has long been recognized that provocations are the only way for the child to express herself to us, saying to the adult, "You still do not see me quite rightly, you still haven't understood me correctly." The moment the child feels accepted, and not judged, but understood, she has the possibility to relax, to quiet down, and to begin to be more attentive and to show a readiness to go in a constructive direction.

The list goes on to mention: healthy and sufficient nutrition; giving the child the feeling that he is protected, valued, loved and sheltered; giving clear boundaries. During the last five years, medical and psychological literature has been singing the praises of giving clear boundaries. That is to say, we should be clear about things we do in a given period of time, there should always be a definite beginning and an end, and there should be clear goals and expectations. That is the new thing now. Do something meaningful in your spare time, no slack. We know now that true, creative play is the only meaningful way to shape your spare time, even when technocrats tell you something different and even when people say that highly gifted children should be given extra challenges. I will come back to this.

There is general awareness of the many dangers that threaten healthy development. To begin with, there is the danger of material poverty. In its wake come poor nutrition, poor medical care, mothers being forced to seek work. This goes together with a low cultural level of the parents, with the danger of cultural antagonism, poor verbal expression, difficult living circumstances, and little opportunity for constructive play. Then there is drug abuse, improper care around the birth, improper understanding of the way children behave . . . all these are great dangers. Furthermore, one-sided tendencies in education pose risks. Extremes that threaten development most are overprotectiveness, neglect (clear enough), and thirdly, praise without discernment. When children experience praise as a lie, because everything is being praised, it means everything and nothing to them, with the result that they lose orientation. Overprotectiveness in education leads to a split: the soul life remains infantile while the demands increase. Intelligence and verbal acuity develop while emotional development remains like that of a small child, narcissistic and demanding. So present-day awareness of the various things that either further or endanger development only needs to be complemented by a better understanding of play. Two new dangers have been added in recent years, which are depression and the readiness to use violence.

Now, where does this so-called acceleration come from? People have occupied themselves a good deal with support for children who are less gifted, much is known about it now, but we don't quite know what to do with children who are highly gifted, nor do we know much about health. During the last ten years there has been an increase in interest in these subjects. Therefore let me give a short introduction to the most essential characteristics. Where does this so-called acceleration come from; what causes this speeding up of development?

First of all we have to mention nutrition. We now know that human mother's milk contains the least amount of protein when compared to all mammals, and also that the human being needs the longest time, compared to all animals, to double his birth weight, namely five months. That is to say, the human being is by nature a slow developer. Why is that necessary for human beings? Why is it always problematic for the human being to learn something very fast and to be able to do things very quickly? The reason for this is that the faster we learn something, the more instinctive and unconscious the learning process will be, and we are invariably less free as a result. When we have had to make a conscious effort to learn something, we have become much more aware of the difficulties which have to be surmounted in learning. A person who has gone through that process will be able to play freely with the acquired ability and inwardly has a more free relationship towards it. In contrast to that, when one has learned something through drill, or under strict guidance, through conditioning, matters are different. This also goes for any behavior that has been trained, or instilled or supported from the outside. Likewise, when a talent is genetically determined, or if one does something from sheer instinct or has a natural gift, there is no free relationship towards that gift or talent. The person who has it just uses it and is surprised that other people don't have it. But at the same time one cannot teach it properly to another person.

Many readers will be able to remember back to a highly gifted math teacher they had in school. Characteristically, such teachers tend to achieve a high level interchange with one-third of the students, while two-thirds of the class is disengaged. A highly gifted teacher simply has great difficulties explaining things to the less gifted, unless she learns how. Because there is only one difference between a higher or lesser degree of talent, which is that someone who is less gifted needs to take a hundred or a thousand little steps before a certain goal is reached, whereas someone who is highly gifted will only need to take a few steps to get to the goal.

And when one doesn't know the small steps, one cannot adapt to the different learning pace different children have. So, please, never feel towards the child, "You poor thing, you poor thing, you are unable to do that." How many times have I heard educators give a systematic list of all the things that a particular child is not able to do. Of course one can list those things. But I would much rather hear, "This child has made this much progress in her language acquisition," or in her dexterity or her color choice for that matter, and what could one do perhaps to support this process; what could the next step be?

We tend to judge quickly and these judgments work in the night. Because thoughts are realities, they work etherically on the children and the children feel branded, judged; they don't feel good. Goethe wrote a wonderful poem to his beloved Frau von Stein, which contains the sentence, "In your eyes I felt good." If we inwardly carry this loving picture of the very special qualities of each child, children will feel understood even when outwardly we have to be strict to them. They will register inwardly, "In his heart of hearts this teacher understands why I flew off the handle again or ruined everything for the others; he knows why I am so unhappy and understands why I react so aggressively."

To illustrate this, here is another small example from the above-quoted stories about children. This excerpt is about one of those aggressive children who can ruin everything.

> *The strength of his being is reflected perhaps most clearly in what happened here. Christoph was easily and often angered and would have outbursts when something didn't go just the way he wanted it. It wasn't uncommon that the children who played with him had to suffer the consequences. It could be quite unpleasant for them when his anger got the better of him. Afterwards he was often sorry that he had hurt the others. One day, after another one of those outbursts, he was sitting in my lap, unhappy and exhausted.*

Now this in itself is important, that children have the feeling that they can turn to somebody when they're doing poorly, that even when they are very unhappy, they know: "Here is somebody who understands me." So that they can say to themselves, "I am not going to crawl into a corner, but I'm going to sit on my kindergarten teacher's lap and interrupt her busy work."

> *He was unhappy about himself. I said to him, "Christoph, now you are so strong." "Yes," he beamed. I said, "Couldn't you try sometimes to be even stronger than your anger?" He looked at me with big eyes. It seemed that he understood me. He was reconciled to himself and went back to play.*

> *It wasn't long before a new opportunity came along to test himself. Two days later he was seized by anger again because something disagreed with him. But this time he didn't knock over what he had just built up and he also didn't yell at his playmates. Instead, he pressed his lips together and energetically started to clear his things away. You could hear how angry he was from the sound of his wooden blocks as he threw them into the basket, and also from the way he stamped his feet, but he*

didn't say anything and clenched his teeth. When all his things had been put away, he was still furious. The children looked at him without saying anything. They were highly amazed, but he didn't notice it. To get rid of the last remainder of his anger, he put up the tables for breakfast and banged the chairs in their places. Then he dropped down on my lap exhausted. "Christoph," I said, "I congratulate you. You were stronger than your anger." He was happy and threw his arms around my neck. From then on he could handle his anger, and soon after there were no more outbreaks.

He felt understood, and when that is the case, things run more smoothly all of a sudden, one can relax. Don't we all know what the circumstances are under which we become intolerable or aggressive? Our threshold drops when we are hungry, tired, when we have relationship problems, when we feel misunderstood. It's that simple.

And in the kindergarten we bring to experience a life in which quietness, nutrition, and understanding for one another are taken care of. To bring this about we have to be sensitive to the way we educate ourselves. A kindergarten teacher who is able to write reports about children such as the one above obviously is in touch with herself, knows her own capacity for anger, knows her own weaknesses and can therefore understand every child's weaknesses. There is no more catastrophic thing than educators who imagine themselves as the teachers who are doing everything right and are wonderful people.

On the contrary, the best educators are those who say, "It comes down to this: we are all wonderful human beings, be it as an ideal, an essence, or as something we can develop into. We must carry this image of one another and confirm each other in our path of development towards this goal. Every weakness which another person has, I have also. I have either conquered it, in which case I can have understanding and be helpful, or I have not yet conquered it, in which case I have a colleague with whom I work on the same thing." People spend lots of money these days on so-called "coaching" programs, in which this very thing is being taught.

So where does acceleration come from? The protein content of our nutrition has increased. Because of this, human beings develop more like animals today. In recent times the human being has been developing faster in body. This is attributed to an increase in the consumption of protein, and also to increased stimulation of the senses, to higher intellectual demands through language and also through corresponding measures to stimulate intelligence. All this stimulates growth of body and intellect. These two always go hand in hand, in contrast to the maturing of the soul, which does not run parallel to the growth of the body and the intellect. And that is where the problem lies, because our happiness primarily depends on whether we feel at home in our souls, whether we look good in our own eyes and in the eyes of others. It depends on the degree to which we can develop a feeling of coherence, as Aaron Antonowski, the creator of the theory of Salutogenesis, calls it. This feeling of coherence is a feeling of connectedness; if one experiences a connection to one's surroundings, life has meaning.

It is for that reason that Rudolf Steiner assigns Waldorf pedagogy basically one single task when he says, "Waldorf pedagogy has the aim to disengage the feeling from the will and connect it to thinking." What does that mean, to disengage the feeling from the will? It is exactly the thing I just read about Christoph. When the will is completely locked in the body and feeling is connected to it, anger automatically leads to an aggressive act. So disconnecting feeling from the will which is bound to the body creates freedom in our relationship with our bodies.

And the most important tools in education to help bring this about are eurythmy and free play. For only in free play will a child learn to grow into his body with her anger, boredom, curiosity, or jealousy in such a way that he can actively begin to get a handle on these feelings — hence the many bad things that can happen when children are already damaged when they enter kindergarten and there have to learn to play. The little child must take this up in such a way that she finds a certain satisfaction in this activity. When children watch others and cannot play well themselves, negative feelings will very soon develop. However, when they become active themselves and feel good about their own will activity, a good sense of self will arise in the body, and that will be a good thing.

When, in addition, the children develop in play and learn to set themselves little tasks, this will promote health because they will learn to handle their will impulses freely, as they connect their own will to their feelings and to their own motivation. And when that happens, the body has to carry out what one would like to do and will no longer react to what comes from outside by means of the senses.

And we practice the other side, that of linking feeling to thinking, when we create a situation for children in which they listen to fairy tales and give them plenty of time to connect themselves through pictures, stories, songs, sounds and sense experiences. In doing so, feeling becomes detached from our own physical bodies and either goes out into the surroundings during the listening activity, or goes out of the body and connects to the world of pictures.

This is just what psychiatrists have been discovering lately in their research. The intelligence of the emotions works on the principle that when feelings accompany observation and thinking, it will be easier to remember what one has thought. The whole problem with memory in our time comes down to a problem of feeling. I will be able to remember the telephone number of a person I'm in love with immediately. Other numbers I may have to write down three times. The difference is as simple as that. I'm emotionally involved with the former, but not with the latter. Feeling also enables one to really identify with something, and can lead to presence of mind (in German *Geistesgegenwart*, literally "spirit presence").

The more the adult is fully there in whatever she is doing, the more attractive, in the truest sense of the word, the magic of the moment will be for the child. This comes about through full involvement of the feelings, both in the adult's presence of mind and in the child's feeling attachment that comes as a result.

In order to bring this development of feeling about, which has to do with the realm of the middle and involves being fully there spiritually, which can only be fully realized in the heart, we need the following three elements. To begin with, strong identification with what one is doing. Second, artistic practice, because that is what awakens, repeats, deepens and strengthens the feelings. And third, fostering a loving connection to the child. For the most beautiful educational measures in the world will be of no avail when this strong, loving connection between educator and child cannot be established.

The theme we have touched here, that of relationship — play — development, really is a threefold constellation which can be a lodestar for us, to such a degree that we can only say, from a medical point of view: Dear Waldorf Movement, dear Waldorf Kindergarten Movement, have faith that this health concept, this concept of development which we are working with, will prove itself more and more in the coming twenty years. People will discover by and by that this is a concept that is in tune with child development. However, you must live this concept and learn to stand for it without being dogmatic or theoretical. A weak spot in our movement is created by cases in which adults do not feel understood by us, but come up against hard judgments. When, instead, we manage to bring the parents into the process of observation and do not enter into defensive debates, we will be able to do much. We are often faced with parents who fear that "the demands are not strict enough, the children are not learning enough, kindergarten is too relaxed." In such cases we must learn to say, "You know, it may seem that way now, but . . ."

Similarly, in the 70s and 80s, we were always being accused of depriving the children of "the freedom of television." In July of 2004 there appeared an article in the internationally renowned medical magazine *The Lancet*, titled "Association Between Children's and Adolescents' Television Viewing and Adult Health: A Longitudinal Birth Cohort Study." 1000 babies were studied for over twenty-six years. It was a completely random selection, talented, untalented, everything, and they were tracked from birth until age twenty-six. Research was done to see how much television they watched and how their state of health was at the end of their twenties. The conclusion was, purely as far as physical health was concerned, that a large percentage of children who sit in front of a screen for between two to four hours daily have weight problems, that they tend to be too fat. In addition it was found that they have heart and lung problems, that physical fitness is less developed, and that they have a tendency to disturbances in the heart rhythm. Furthermore, it was found that their serum cholesterol levels are too high, that they have a much stronger disposition to smoking, to alcohol, to drug consumption and that their average blood pressure is too high. This of course is connected to the cholesterol.

No mention has been made yet of the psychological damage, of course. But I think it's a great thing that such studies are being published at all now, even though they have not yet translated into pedagogical practice. Such an example shows that what Waldorf pedagogy emphasized at the rise of television, beginning in the 50s and 60s, has now been scientifically proven, thirty to fifty years later. It is our duty to regard these scientific data with great modesty and gratitude, because it wasn't we who did the research, and we can now use them to strengthen the foundation of our work. At the same time, this research can fill us with great joy and we can be grateful that anthroposophy has given us access to a concept of healthy human development that is a result of spiritual research. Even though there is no systematic proof as yet, we can freely acknowledge the correctness of the insights of spiritual science, which enable us to do the right thing, so we need not wait another hundred years until everything has been researched. This is a form of grace. We can be glad for it and this awareness can give us strength.

To close, I would like to read words written by Karl Schubert, the special education teacher of whom Rudolf Steiner was so fond.

By the power of the word we can lift in the physical, heal in the etheric, forgive in the astral, console in the ego.

In the morning, when we call the children by name, our use of the word gives them uprightness. It strengthens their identity and it helps them in their incarnation. But as we speak and tell stories, nourishing the etheric, we foster the world of pictures inasmuch as we bring them into a restful and orderly sequence. And as we master difficult situations in the kindergarten by the use of our words, dealing with problems and emotional outbursts in such a way that forgiveness and understanding play in, with forgiveness coming about through understanding, we bring peace and healing to the injured souls of the children of our time. And this consolation in the ego: we should always be aware in our egos, and convey this feeling to the children, that we are friends in our relationship from I to I. On that level we are friends; we can comfort each other, and help each other.

The Formative Forces and the Threshold of the Second Seven-Year Period

CHRISTOF WIECHERT

I want to try to describe the transition from the kindergarten to the lower school in terms of the relation of teachers to children, and then I would like to offer another anecdote that expresses something you will recognize immediately. We remember the wonderful story told by Joan Almon: a bit tragic, but nevertheless very impressive, the story of the boy in her kindergarten who played with crocheted ropes and, in my interpretation, imprisoned himself and his friend in these ropes. And then she found a solution.

Children under seven, or under six — Steiner never said it must be precisely seven, always when he talks about this transition, he speaks about six, seven — the child before six or seven has to learn to find himself in the flow of time and in the structure of space. And we as kindergarten teachers need the strength to, in a human way, organize the flow of time and the structure of space, so that the child can find himself. So the kindergarten teacher, out of her ego, organizes time and space, and the child can find himself. She must apply her ego forces and humanize the space. She has formative forces to make this possible in physical reality. Now, what did Joan Almon do? She "only" rearranged something in physical reality, she put away the basket with the ropes, and when the boy asked for it, she said very simply without any argument, "The ropes have to rest." "Okay," said the boy. Her action physically structured the room so that he could no longer play his imprisonment game with the ropes. In order to achieve this, she needed an idea, an impulse, perhaps an inspiration, or maybe it was even much simpler than that. In any case, she *did* something.

Now, imagine that someone else is confronted with this same problem. Perhaps this person (no one here in this room of course!) says to the boy the next morning, "You know, it's not healthy to do that. I think that you are showing that you feel imprisoned. Go play something else instead." I guess that psychologically this is not so good. We laugh, because we feel it's nonsense to act like that. But be aware that this is what happens in the mainstream of education today. If we start the schooling processes, as is now the practice in some countries, at three years of age, then this is how we work in the kindergarten. This is the reality of life in many kindergartens.

Now I will give you a similar example from the reality of life in the lower school. It happened not far from here last year that a first grade teacher had a class of thirty-five children, and things went along as they do, with everyone happy, except for one terribly difficult boy. He could not listen, he could not imitate, he was quite terrible. The teacher suffered a great deal over this, feeling that all the energy needed to bring joy into the class was drained out of her. She had no idea what to do.

And then, at the end of the school day, she met a colleague, and she started to talk with her about this boy. And this colleague, who was a bit older, listened very carefully, and suddenly she felt how the focus of the discussion shifted from this boy to herself. And through this discussion with her colleague, she received an impression, a picture of her own antipathy. She had suddenly this picture that she had built a wall between herself and this boy. And she felt: "Because there is this wall, he will not become better, but worse and worse." They finished their discussion without any solution. The next morning this boy came into the first grade classroom with a little bouquet of spring flowers and said, "For you." And the problems were finished. So try to understand this. It is not possible as Herbert Marcuse says, through one-dimensional thinking.

What happened? From her soul, from her soul searching, she worked on the formative qualities of this boy. The blessing in the situation was that she could endure the discussion with her colleague, and that this colleague asked the right question, not a judgment, but just the right question. She described the situation as a powerful healing of herself.

Steiner, on two occasions, described the outcome of child study — please, don't misunderstand this word — as "white magic." We, through our souls, work in such a way that the soul of the child is touched, and from his soul he can work into his formative, into his etheric reality.

So the class teacher has to become the genius of soul. The kindergarten teacher has to develop himself or herself to become the genius of the etheric. That's the main difference. Naturally — so that there is no misunderstanding — we need the relationship of the entire human being, but I do believe that there is an astonishing difference. The kindergarten teacher, according to her own possibilities, organizes time and space so that the physical reality can realize itself. The class teacher organizes out of his soul powers the inner possibilities for the strengthening of the formative forces. And in our times, this is not an easy task. I'll give you an example.

A few months ago, a colleague of mine, in northern Germany, started his third cycle of classes from one to eight. And as it should be, after every cycle he had had a year off, a sabbatical, and began in September with his new first grade class. Wonderful children, joyful, nice, special children. And then came Christmas. You know how it is in social organizations — with Christmas, you have to work to make it happen. It doesn't come by itself. So the two weeks before Christmas are not always the easiest ones. So my colleague was at the edge of losing his temper — not really, but nearly. One little boy looked at him, and he said to him, "Do you need another sabbatical?" And another boy said to him from the other side, "And I have to live with you for eight years!" He is very good, this teacher. The second boy came the next day to him and when it was time to say "Good morning," he said to the teacher, "The eight years will be okay!"

How do we cope with such things? We know that children today awaken earlier and earlier, but how do we speak about this, and how do we deal with it? I would like to explore this theme a bit further. How do we do this? I have a "crazy" suggestion: "Don't be dogmatic." When my colleague heard this boy say, "Do you need another sabbatical," if he had been dogmatic, he would have immediately phoned the parents (that is a specialty in Waldorf schools though I hope not in kindergartens) and he would have said to the mother, "Your son needs immediate psychological help, because of what he said to me. It was totally unacceptable!" This example is not hypothetical!

I heard another amazing but tragic story yesterday, like Joan's story of how the boy with the ropes, when he was grown up, had serious problems with a kind of network spread across the whole globe. This is the story I heard yesterday. A mother was absolutely happy with her child in the Waldorf school. The child developed wonderfully, and all went well, and finally the boy was in eighth grade. The mother was a very good mother but also a journalist, and as you know, journalists are often of a certain character. The eighth grade class teacher said that the children had to wear slippers in school, because it was more hygienic. A good reason. However, this boy just had gotten his first wonderful bright brilliant shining Nikes, and he didn't want to change his Nikes for the slippers. Yet the teacher knew that of course he was right, and he said: "Slippers." And you know how it is: if the teacher says "slippers" then the boy could only say "No!" "But you must!" said the teacher. "No!" said the boy. And then the journalist in the mother awoke, and a week later, the boy had left school. There was no flexibility, and there is a basic rule: "We, as teachers, must always be more flexible than parents." That's a rule of professionalism. We have to be more flexible than parents because we are not the teachers of the parents.

Let's go back to this transition between the first and the second seven-year period. I will pose a strange question, in order to arrive at a certain idea. I'm sure that in this room are hundreds of colleagues who were intellectually educated before they were seven. And they are still normal people and good colleagues. That's a reality. Can we understand that? And now I will try to make it understandable [*Herr Wiechert draws on the blackboard*]. Here we have the human being, and here we have his threefold organization, which you know from your anthroposophical studies, which are the wellspring and the source of our well-being in this profession, by the way. We know that up to the age of six or seven, the formative forces that stream through the head from out of the cosmos organize the child in space and time. And around six, seven, sometimes a bit earlier, these forces are ready, and they come back, and these forces are still flowing, streaming. So there is an encounter of formative forces that stream back, and formative forces that stream in. And out of this encounter, which Steiner called a "battlefield," we have the change of teeth. In this process, in our intellectual possibilities, we organize our selves through the quality and the capacities that are available to us.

This is the birth of the formative forces, but there were also formative forces before. And in the head, there are particular formative forces, very special ones. Steiner describes them in a lecture about memory; these formative forces in the head (not those freed through the second birth) are free to be used from birth and do not have to use their forces for growth. I will try to make this understandable.

Through the eurythmy we saw this morning, or if we look at these colored windows here in the Great Hall, we have an impression. We can be only aware of this impression if we have an astral body, if we have a soul body. So we are aware of these colored windows through our soul. The moment we close our eyes, and we see an inner picture, a memory image, it's not the soul anymore but the etheric body, the etheric force, that creates the picture.

There is very interesting research done on the pictorial memory of little children, small children between two and six years old. The study is difficult to carry out, because it requires that children be able to make drawings of their memories. If we show a three- or four-year-old child a certain image or a star, he is able to have a mental picture (in German *Vorstellung*), an inner image of that what he has seen. And these are the etheric forces, a portion of the etheric body that never was used to organize the child's relationship to time and space. These forces were free from the beginning.

This etheric quality is quite strong. Steiner said about this etheric quality that we should use it for our learning through games and play, and also for learning processes. To be precise, this portion of the etheric forces that are not used for the growth of the human being can be used for learning processes.

Now we can understand that Steiner said, "If we do it in a normal way, in a human way, we can teach foreign languages even in the kindergarten." Maybe the word teaching is wrong, but let's say it in this way, that even in the kindergarten we can work with foreign languages. Then we are not ruining the children's etheric forces, those that are freed in the second birth, and make possible the relation between our pictorial experience and our mental picturing, where our intellect arises, where memory is sharpened and individualized. Because if we use this part of the etheric forces earlier, it is not individualized. And when what we then learn is not individualized, it shows up in a child in a tragic or humorous way. When a first grader says to his teacher "Do you need a second year off?" it's humorous. Why? Because such an expression has not been individualized; it is an expression that has not yet gone through the soul. It can become tragic, if we give children tasks in grammar or have them write mathematical solutions, teach them to read, and so on. Then their ability to learn is overburdened and the child cannot offer something that has gone through his soul. There is no humor here — it has become a matter of achievement.

There is another thing I'd like to draw your attention to. On a certain occasion, Steiner said: "It is true that we think with our brain. You know real anthroposophists don't think with their brains. They think with their etheric forces." That's no joke. If thinking is a reality, it is a thought quality related to the brain. I mentioned earlier the founder of the "One-dimensional Man," Herbert Marcuse. Where our thoughts can only grasp what we see, what we can control, what we can be sure about, then we have the tragic side of these etheric forces. But we know that much more often Steiner said that the most important task in kindergarten and in the lower school and upper school is to enliven human thinking. Bring life into your thoughts, bring them into movement, fill them with life, and bring them into relation with the powers of imagination, of fantasy.

This step takes place in the University of Play, since children in kindergarten and in the early years of the Waldorf school are in the university of their play time. There all these capacities are combined — the quality of the life processes and the sensory processes. To make it perfectly clear: it is possible to have some learning processes already in the kindergarten. It is possible. I have had several children in my first grade classes who, because they had elder brothers and sisters were already able to read and write. And they entered the school and said, "What shall I learn?" And I said, "Oh, wait, and we will see." And then, very quickly, because it wasn't individualized, they forgot what they had learned, and they started again, like new. That is possible.

Now, if we have Waldorf schools, if we have kindergartens, in countries where learning is approached intellectually at an early age, then we will have to find solutions. I'm sure that we will find a way in the foreseeable future to humanize this, to find a way to utilize these etheric forces of the head very carefully. When we play, we prepare the birth of the individualized etheric forces. So I think the only thing to do in such a difficult situation is to do what we can, what we learn, what we can do out of anthroposophy, namely, to individualize. It is better to have a child wearing "Nikes" in your class than a child without slippers outside school. We have a huge social task.

Between the sixth and seventh year, there is a birth, and at the same time it is not a birth, today it is a fluid transitional period. I will give you an example. I once had a little girl in class one. She was much, much too tall and very slim. I learned quickly that that was out of heredity, for her mother and her father were just as tall. But you could immediately feel that she wasn't able to live in her body. Climbing a staircase was a real problem. She had to pull herself up the stairs. And when she walked it was as if she were walking on ice. I didn't know what to do, and she was absolutely not ready to learn. So she sat there looking at me with her big blue eyes and I thought: "Oh, God, what shall I do?" When we played circle games and danced and recited poems and riddles and so on, she was not able to follow. So I let her sit on the chair, and she looked on, and I thought: "I need a specialist." And at that moment, I remembered that Steiner said that the Waldorf school, till eighth grade, until children are fourteen years old, is not a place for specialists; it is a place for human beings. But I didn't know what to do.

If you don't know what to do, you start something and have trust in your own action. So I took her to the play yard next to the school, and around the border of the play yard are huge stone blocks, with spaces between. And I said to her, "I will teach you to jump from block to block, from rock to rock." They were flat, you know. And all that was painful. Her hand cramped in my hand. But we did it every day at recess, and then we made a game out of it with the whole class. They all tried to jump from block to block. And then she hesitated: "Shall I, or shall I not?" and hop! She did it. And we all applauded: "Fantastic, Barbara!"

And then with classmates, we did walking slowly up and down the stairways, and then a bit faster, and then fast, with a child on each hand. After two or three years, she was well incarnated in her body and absolutely normal, also her speech. Speech and singing are movements which are modified and directly inward; these "movements" are threatened today. According to a survey in Germany, four out of ten six-year-old children have speech problems; here great challenges await us in terms of overall movement development.

Now, you can say: "Oh, that is the task for the kindergarten." Maybe, but on the other hand, she was six, seven years old when she came to first grade. So our task for the future is to bring more kindergarten elements into the lower school in first and second grade, and maybe bring some grade school elements into the kindergarten. Some schools already have a beginners' class, a class between kindergarten and first grade. I hope it is an experiment and that there are some countries who will say, we have already been doing that for years. It is an attempt, this in-between class. For the future, and this future starts now, we need to be more flexible and open in taking children that are not precisely our imagination of the "right" child, if you understand what I mean. There is a little danger in the Waldorf movement that we expect a child to be as our picture of him is. But a child should be as he is himself, and I have to train myself to see him as he is, to take hold of him, and to develop him.

Dear friends, it is so wonderful and at the same time we are at war, a war that is waging behind the scenes of visibility. There a battle is taking place. The question is: will the free human being be able, be allowed, to keep the forces of his childhood and work on them and use them throughout his lifetime? In a lecture given by Rudolf Steiner before he was no longer allowed to speak because of National Socialism, because of the brown hordes, at this last occasion he gave his listeners a verse — a verse which is still very relevant today:

> To bind one's soul to matter, is to grind souls to dust.
> To find oneself in the spirit, is to unite human beings.
> To behold oneself in the human being, is to build worlds.

This is our task, one that we can take up, and one we can do better and better each day.

The Encounter with Human and Spiritual Beings

DR HEINZ ZIMMERMANN

I would like to recall a few things we have experienced together during this week. This conference had "Playing, learning, meeting the other" for a theme. At one point, one of the lecturers talked about the long lines we had to deal with before we were able to get to the food, and I believe that actual meetings did take place in those long lines. Perhaps connections were made which will go into the future. So those were meetings that took place during the breaks.

Breaks are in fact the most important thing in conferences, so henceforth we should only organize conferences to have opportunities for breaks. That's where you meet people, where contacts are made, and where everything is unplanned, in contrast to situations like this where someone stands in front of you, and you more or less know what to expect. But during the breaks things are different. And I hope that many fruitful meetings, friendships, connections and exchanges have come about between people from all over the world. Just imagine, people will now go south, north, west, east, back to work, taking with them everything they have experienced during the breaks. They will bring the whole world with them.

Now we will briefly look back on the morning lectures. Rather than trying to summarize all the content which was brought, I will focus on some things which seemed essential to me.

This morning we heard two impressive phrases from Christof Wiechert. First, "Do it better in your own place." The source of all change is the place where I work. It is a terrible thing to have the feeling "I have to change the whole world." There's no end in sight when you think that way. But I will change everything when I work in my own place, when I have impulses to do something different and new right where I am. Another thing he said was "Don't be dogmatic." What is being dogmatic? Being dogmatic is sitting on the seat of one's judgments and always knowing beforehand how things really are. "Rudolf Steiner said . . ." — that's another form of being dogmatic, when one doesn't look at how things are. Things may be quite different from what one had thought. Dogmatism always has to do with how things were, but we need to be in the present. So, "don't be dogmatic," and "create what you need in your own place."

Now we come to Peter Selg. "Our treasure is where our heart is." A beautiful phrase. What is dear to us, that is where our heart lies. And this brings us to the motive of Waldorf pedagogy. We are looking for the spirit of the middle, the spirit of the heart, and the heart cannot beat in isolation. It cannot work when head and limbs are not involved. The heart must be able to mediate something; it gives impulses in two directions, up and down. The heart forms the middle between head and limbs, and the spirit of the middle is such that equilibrium is never a stable thing, but has to be sought anew at every point. Every step we take brings us out of balance, and the next step must restore that balance again. That is the secret of walking upright. This touches on the secret that the human being is upright, and must go the path of seeking balance, which is not a given. The search for the middle is an ongoing quest.

Next came Michaela Glöckler with the theme of acceleration and retardation. We must have trust in the effectiveness of our pedagogy, and have faith that what seems small has a big future. It is indeed a major problem that we always have the feeling that we are a laughable minority in the face of the power of present-day circumstances, that we are puny. But we are as puny as a sunflower seed in a very big sunflower. The sunflower seed is there so that there can be another sunflower next year. We have to cultivate the seed, and the seed is always inconspicuous. But the whole future lies in the seed. What has grown in the past and is now established is mighty indeed, but new growth is tender like the little child, and we are called to tend this seed. We must trust the effectiveness of the pedagogy of Rudolf Steiner.

Now we come to Joan Almon. We looked with her at the darkness of our time. There are these frightful statistics with numbers one can hardly face, showing how play is on the wane with every passing year. And play is nothing but a message from the world before birth, out of which the little child comes to us. In the activity of free play, children reveal something of this highly tender world before birth, which we can see beautifully expressed in the purple window in this hall. What is demanded of us? On the one hand we must continue in our efforts to bring the light of this pedagogy to the fore and make it shine. Next to that: "Have the courage to nurture free play and to represent it." So: "Have the courage to stand for it and to say: that's the essential thing, that is where our humanity lies." Over against a world of destruction we must have the courage to say something that cannot boast as big a success as winning a soccer game. We are in a situation where we have many opponents, which would rather see that humanity does not develop. In this context we can also add the sentence: "Make yourself available as an expert." You are representatives of a future pedagogy of humanity, whether you are conscious of that fact or not; that is what you are for the world. And the better you can fulfill that role as a representative, the more effective this pedagogy will be.

My own lecture was adequately reviewed in the skit yesterday evening, so not much more need be added. Instead, I would like to still focus on a second phrase from Michaela Glöckler: "Meet the child where she is." Where might that be? Let's make this clear to ourselves: Where is the little child? Where is the child whom we have to educate? When we can answer this question, we will also know how to meet that child and how to give shape to this meeting. The little child comes from the spiritual sphere of life before birth, and as educators we should conceive of ourselves as continuing the work that higher beings have done for the child before birth — an incredible perspective. We are working together with spiritual powers.

And when we take this phrase, "meeting the child where she is," we have to learn something of this world before birth, not only in a theoretical sense but also in practice. The philosopher Plato expressed a tremendous thought when he asked the question, "What in fact is learning?" — which is part of the theme of this conference about meeting, learning and playing. Learning, says Plato, is nothing but remembering what was experienced before birth. And teachers are people who are there to make conscious what already lives inside the children. The point is not to fill the children with knowledge about civilization, but to bring out this treasure from the spiritual world before birth, so that the child will remember what her task is in the world. It's a wonderful thought that "learning is remembering what was there in a sphere that I once inhabited and have to learn again in this incarnation, step by step." Here again it is quite clear that the ruler of this world is only too interested in replacing this kind of learning with a type of learning which kills these impulses, in order to adapt it to a world that we in fact would like to change with all our might.

So what is this realm before birth? What is it like? It is a realm where things are coming into being, a realm that just borders the sense world. When we do exercises such as the one Joan Almon mentioned, the exercise of "growing — blossoming followed by perishing — withering," we will become able to take a step into the realm of the elements, the first supersensible realm, in which the formative forces are active which build up the child. It is a world in which everything is in a state of becoming, and we have the task of receiving it and integrating it gradually into this world of things which "have become," so that it doesn't perish.

It is also the world of rhythm, the world of movement, and last Wednesday we could perceive it in the eurythmy and also in the musical presentations. We could hear in the music: this is the world of the elementary formative forces, what could be called "the world of the periphery," the world where things come to meet us from out of the future. And anyone who has experienced it will also have noticed that those are forces that renew us, forces that make us fresher than we were before. In eurythmy, in music, and in art, we are in the realm of the life forces, where the well-springs of existence are at work. Here we meet the gnomes, the dwarfs, the spirits of water and air, Undines and Sylphs such as the ones we saw here on the stage. When we saw them like that, we could experience that no one would ask whether such things really exist. On the contrary, one could sense: "That's a reality from which our sense-perceptible world springs." We are surrounded by what has been created, and from this world it is a step to enter into the realm of the etheric.

This same realm is the world of movement. Everything is in movement. This too you have proven during these days, especially last evening in front of the Goetheanum and around it, that we can meet another human being in movement only through our own movement; we must be moving ourselves. The more we as human beings enter into movement, the more spiritual we become. We could really define spirit as movement. And you know how it is when you want to observe movement. It is pretty difficult. The moment you want to catch it, it has passed. For example, when you want to look at eurythmy and ask yourself, "What is every single individual doing at this point? Where is this one, and where the other?" Especially when it is a fast piece, you feel you can't do it, you'll get dizzy. When you come to the realization that you're actually inside the realm of movement, only then will you enter the sphere of eurythmy and sense how you are refreshed. When you set yourself in motion, you can enter that world of movement.

Now, there is a part of the human being that retards this, namely the head. It brings movement to rest. That is its task, after all. It is a very bad thing when the head is too strong and there is no more movement and too much sitting, a culture of sitting («*Sitz*»-*kultur*). Then the Waldorf movement, and likewise the anthroposophical movement, stands in danger of being no longer a movement but a session (*Sitzung*). But now we come to the way back, the counter-stream of time, by which I mean the effort of not only moving the limbs, and not only moving the heart rhythmically in repetition, but of bringing into movement again what the head first had to quieten down. That doesn't mean shaking one's head, but a more inward process. It means bringing something in motion again which first had to be dampened in order for us to come to ego-consciousness, a process that took place in puberty.

Our thinking, which is spatial, and must be so in the realm of "finished" creation, operates in terms of either/or. This is thinking by means of definitions, and in order to come to any definition I first have to dampen the living process. This dampening is actually a form of killing. When I want to define a person, a child, and say, "This child is such and such," I have killed him by means of my thinking. I should say, now the child is like this, but he will develop, perhaps in quite a different way from what I imagine at this moment. In other words: I have to develop a kind of thinking which encompasses "both/and," which grasps that one thing develops out of another. And as soon as one enters the realm of living thinking, one notices that thinking and moving do not contradict one another but are two sides of the same thing.

One could say we have seen living concepts on stage, in the eurythmy, and when we really practice living thinking, we are performing eurythmy inside. It is one and the same thing, it involves forming and releasing in the stream of time, in such a way that one thinks out of the future and not out of the past. And this is the only way to really reach the child adequately, because the child is so close to this world of the etheric, to the realm before birth. We have to set ourselves in motion in our limbs, our hearts and our thinking.

This movement-character which goes right into thinking, one could say, also comes to expression in play, which is a holy thing to children. They devote themselves to it with such earnestness. What is children's play? It is nothing less than a message from before birth, carried out here on earth. As they play, children continue something for which we must create space. It is our first priority to guard this free space. The earnest, devoted play of the child, which must unfold freely, is thus the model for the free play of the adult, who plays between the requirements of the sense world and the laws of the spirit. "Through the senses to the spirit" is what our education is about. That is the source of our pedagogy.

We now come to yet another perspective on how we meet the child. How do we meet the child "where she is"? The nearness of the prenatal world requires a basic attitude in us, which we have right in front of us in little children. They give us the example. When we look into the eyes of a three- or four-year-old with this open trust in the world, we can see how the child says from the depth of her being, "This world is good. I can imitate it."

How can we meet this boundless trust? Only by meeting the world with the same attitude which the child has by nature.

I would like to call this attitude a fundamentally religious one. Of course this word is fraught with misunderstandings. The word religious imme-diately makes one think "Christian," or " Muslim," or a particular de-nomination. The word evokes church and incense and so on, but all this is not what is meant here. If we observe the small child, we have the basic tenor of religiosity right in front of our eyes. For the child cannot but look up. Adults are simply bigger, in a physical sense to begin with. The child always looks up. When we imagine, if only for a moment, that we look up at a table, or an older person, or at a face from the perspective of a child, all we need to do is to transpose that situation to a soul-spiritual level.

When we look up at the stars the way we were able to do last night — how wonderful that we could experience that! — we also enter a mood which could be called religious. We become quiet and look with reverence into an exalted world, where we can see both the endless movement and endless quietude of the cosmos, and we experience not only how we look at the stars, but how the stars are looking at us. We thus enter into the mood of devotion, we have reverence for something higher and we come into contact with beings who are higher than we are ourselves. This is the basic mood of prayer. And the shift into the world that the child recently came from is at the same time a way of cultivating a religious mood, a culture of prayer.

This can happen when we meet another person. In such meetings we can have moments where we sense something of an understanding living between us that is of such a nature that we cannot even express it in words. And after such a meeting one can sense how one has not only seen that human being in an earthly form, but discovered something infinite and divine. When such experiences occur, words stop; those kinds of moments one can only guard and be faithful to. And likewise there can be moments, flashes, in meeting the little child, where you feel you meet a wisdom that is much higher than you are.

With regard to the topic of cultivating an attitude of prayer as we do in kindergarten and in fact during the first seven years altogether, we should note that this can go hand in hand with a down-to-earth attitude. There is no contradiction between the two. The poet Hölderlin used the words *heilig-nuechtern* ("holy — down-to-earth"). It is not a sentimental attitude, but it is *heilig-nuechtern*. Heraclitus, one of the Pre-Socratic philosophers, said, "God is a playing child." For me this is a most wonderful saying, "God is a playing child." The playing child brings creative powers to expression. And when we manage to look up to the forces at work in the zodiac, with its twelve signs, and the sphere of the seven planets, where we can recognize the powers of the Logos, the shaping powers of the cosmic word out of which everything is created, we can recognize that it is this world to which we have to regularly and rhythmically seek a connection.

The world of the supersensible also gives us strength and enables us to meet in a completely different way. This also includes meeting completely different people and regions of the world. It is the type of meeting which we could experience so wonderfully during this week, in the reports from the different countries, in the meetings during the breaks, in the presentations in different languages. These different cultures, languages, and religious convictions made it possible for the whole world to be present like a cosmos during one short week. In this we could sense the cosmopolitan impulse. In religious terms we could say: we look through the lens of Buddha, the lens of Krishna, the lens of Jehovah, and the lens of Mohammed. In whatever cultural setting we find ourselves with regards to religion, we get a glimpse of a shaping power, which is connected to the sun we all share, the spirit sun that gives us the strength of the middle.

This is much too great and all-encompassing a force, and also much too intimate, to give a single name to, for it comprises something cosmopolitan. It spans the whole world and transcends all religions and nationalities, and is connected to the spirit of our time. We can also give the name "Michael" to this spirit of our time, even though that is not essential. This spirit of the time conquers all differences, everything which places us into a certain landscape, social connection, and so on. All these things can be conquered by the sun, radiating out of the future, uniting all differences. And one can say we have all this in caricature today in our globalization, in our ability to communicate with our cell phones, which can be heard everywhere, whether the time is right or not, and by means of which we can communicate with anybody at any time. We form a unity all around the globe. We are human beings by virtue of the fact that we say "I" to ourselves, regardless of the color of our skin, religion, or nationality. And to foster this is the original intent out of which anthroposophy has grown; it is also the reason why this place was created as the Goetheanum. This place was meant to be a place where people from all over the world can meet in the spirit of the middle, in the Sun Spirit, to whom this building has been dedicated.

Every day this week we started our work with the simple and wonderful children's prayer "From my head to my feet." Our educational movement of the human middle is likewise founded in a prayer. It is a prayer that starts from the premise that we will not be able to fulfill our task at all when we do not connect ourselves with higher beings, every day anew. That is the foundation stone that has been laid for this pedagogy in the form of a prayer, a threefold prayer.

We are individuals to begin with, each having our individual destiny that is embedded in a larger network of destiny. What we need today for our work comes out of this living world of being-ness, which we have attempted to approach during this week, and it is to this world we turn when we ask our higher self, our guardian angel, to give us the necessary strength.

Yet we need something more. Not only do we live in the powerlessness of our individual situation, we also live in a world full of fear. And who can say of himself that he is completely free from this fear and could invariably say, "No problem — the world is good, things will come right"? When one has not reached the point of not knowing how to go on, one will not be able to ask for courage in the right sense of the word. We are not just asking for individual courage here. At this point we turn to an even higher being in the world of the hierarchies, we pray to a being from the realm of the archangels, the spirits of community. Every one of us, wherever we are, is embedded in a world of connections, be it connections with parents, children, or all those who advocate for us and take an interest in us. Our destinies are united and we have a communal destiny, especially in a school.

Our school is guided by a spirit, and woe to us if we disregard what that spirit stands for. This spirit, too, must be nurtured, and it is to this spirit that we turn and ask for courage, courage through and for our work together, for working towards the common goal.

Imagine we would confine ourselves to being good educators and also good colleagues. That would not suffice, something would be missing. We might have the notion that it would be possible to have a wonderful kindergarten on a flowering island, away from this terrible time, where we have to say, "We want no computer, we want no television, we want no soccer, we want no chewing gum."

Isn't it unbelievable, how often we say what we don't want? Our children, however, have decided to come to this world where all those things are, and they want to overcome it. We have to connect with that, and that brings us to the third thing we ask and pray for. We have the task to accept the world the way it is, and to work with these children the way they are. To accomplish that we need a spiritual light. Everywhere where there are large shadows, there will be a large source of light. That is a physical law: where there is shadow, there also is light.

And when we try to turn to this light, we reach the sphere of the spirit who guides the destiny of our time throughout the world, and here we do so in view of free play, of freedom, and of courage. This has to do with the realm of the time-spirit Michael, with that light which causes the shadows and challenges us to overcome them.

A wonderful teachers' prayer was noted down from memory, and you can read the exact text in the book *Zur Vertiefung der Waldorfpädagogik* ("Towards the Deepening of Waldorf Pedagogy"), published by the Pedagogical Section. We ask the angel, who accompanies us as the guardian of our individual destiny, for strength. We turn to the circle of the archangels, to the spirit of community, and ask for courage, and ask this spirit to build a vessel of this courage through the community, a vessel into which a drop of light falls out of the realm of the spirit of our time, Michael. By ourselves we feel powerless, and from out of this feeling we ask for strength from the angel; from out of a world of fright and fear we ask the community spirit for courage; and we ask for light from the spirit of our times from out of a world of darkness, which we experience daily.

When one imagines that hundreds and hundreds of men and women working in education connect themselves every day, morning and evening, with this world of strength-giving, hierarchical energy — what strength this gives! It is a strength that doesn't come from the world of the senses, but is germinal strength from the heart to work for a pedagogy of the middle.

In this sense I wish you courage, strength, and light for your work, and thank you for coming to the Goetheanum, the House of the Word, because the ideals of anthroposophy, of the School for Spiritual Science, for which this Goetheanum stands, are the same ideals as those of our art of education. In this sense, therefore, greetings also from the Spirit of the Goetheanum.

Biographical notes

JOAN ALMON was born in 1944 in Wilmington, Delaware, USA. She completed a BA in sociology at the University of Michigan; graduate courses in Waldorf education through Towson State University, Maryland. Joan became a Waldorf kindergarten teacher at the beginning of the 1970s. After twenty years she began to visit Waldorf kindergartens all over the world, in North America, Africa, and Asia, among others. She was on the Board of the Waldorf Early Childhood Association of North America and a member of the Kuratorium of the International Waldorf Kindergarten Association. She has served as Coordinator of the Alliance for Childhood in the United States and one of the two General Secretaries of the Anthroposophical Society of America. Publications include articles about childhood and play in numerous magazines, both inside and outside the Waldorf movement, and books including *First Steps in Natural Dyeing*. She is currently an international early childhood consultant and serves on the board of the Alliance for Childhood.

MICHAELA GLÖCKLER was born in 1946 in Stuttgart, Germany. She studied medicine in Tübingen and Marburg, and then specialized in pediatrics at the Community Hospital in Herdecke and the University Clinic in Bochum. She was a practicing pediatrician and school doctor for ten years. Since Easter of 1988 she has led the Medical Section of the School for Spiritual Science at the Goetheanum in Dornach, Switzerland. Publications include *Elternsprechstunde* ("Consultations with parents"), *Elternfragen heute* ("Questions parents have today"), *Medizin an der Schwelle* ("Medicine at the threshold"), *Das Schulkind* ("The child in school"), *Heilkraft der Religion* ("The healing power of religion"), and *Spirituelle Ethik* ("Spiritual ethics"). Publications available in English: *A Guide to Child Health* (with Wolfgang Goebel); *A Healing Education*; *Medicine at the Threshold of a New Consciousness*.

CHRISTOF WIECHERT was born in 1945 and attended the Waldorf school in The Hague, the Netherlands. After studying pedagogy and geography, he taught for thirty years at the Waldorf school in The Hague. During this time he was co-founder of the State-recognized Waldorf teacher training in the Netherlands. For many years he was on the Board of the Dutch anthroposophical society. Christof served as Heinz Zimmerman's successor as the Leader of the Pedagogical Section until his retirement in 2011. He continues to be involved in the work of the Section as an international teacher trainer, lecturer and consultant, and in 2012 he authored a book called *Teaching, The Joy of Profession: An Invitation to Enhance Your (Waldorf) Interest*, published by the Verlag am Goetheanum. Together with Ate Koopmans he developed the course "The Art of Child Study." He lectures frequently at home and abroad.

HEINZ ZIMMERMANN was born in 1937 in Basel, Switzerland. He attended the Waldorf school there, and studied German, history and philology of ancient languages at the University of Basel. In 1964, he acquired a PhD with a dissertation on "The Typology of Spontaneous Conversation." From 1965–66 he worked for the Goethe Institute in Finland, then became an assistant and later a lecturer in German philology at the University of Basel. For twenty-five years he was a teacher at the Waldorf school in Basel, teaching German, History, History of Art, and Latin. In 1975 he joined the faculty of the Waldorf teacher training in Dornach. In 1988 he was called to join the Vorstand of the General Anthroposophical Society and was leader of the Pedagogical Section from 1989 until 2001. From 1992 until 1999 he led the Youth Section. He later carried responsibility for the Basic Studies in Anthroposophy and the Individual Study Program at the Goetheanum and continued to act as an international advisor on Waldorf education, especially in the realm of meditation and the inner life of the teacher, until his death in 2011.

Made in the USA
Charleston, SC
03 October 2012